teenage STRESS
A Guide for Teenagers

Dr Charmaine Saunders

SALLY MILNER PUBLISHING

First published in 1992 by
Sally Milner Publishing Pty Ltd
558 Darling Street
Rozelle NSW 2039 Australia

© Charmaine Saunders 1992

Production by Sylvana Scannapiego,
Island Graphics
Typeset in Australia by Asset Typesetting Pty Ltd
Printed in Australia by Australian Print Group

National Library of Australia
Cataloguing-in-Publication data:

Saunders, Charmaine.
 Teenage stress.

 ISBN 1 86351 088 5.

 1. Stress in adolescence. 2. Stress (Psychology).
 3. Teenagers — Health and hygiene. I. Title.
 (Series: Milner healthy living guide).

155.90420835

All rights reserved. No part of this publication may be
reproduced, stored in a retrieval system or transmitted in
any form or by any means, electronic, mechanical,
photocopying, recording or otherwise, without prior
written permission of the copyright owners and publishers.

Teenage Stress

Teenagers live in a world of change and confusion. There are stress traps in family life, school, work, relationships, just growing up. More than every today, young people need help and guidance to get them through the years between childhood and adulthood. Teenage suicide is on the increase, youth unemployment is at an all-time high, family life is breaking down. How do we teach teenagers to stay positive through all these challenges?

Dr Charmaine Saunders is a columnist, teacher and counsellor who has worked with young people for over twenty years. In this, her third stress book, she offers practical strategies, positive advice and down-to-earth ideas about teenage life, both for parents and teenagers themselves. Through case studies, anecdotes, examples and exercises, she leads the reader with humour, warmth and, most importantly, hope.

This book is a must for all teenagers, their parents and anyone who has a professional and personal interest in the welfare of young people and their future role in society.

About the Author

Charmaine Saunders has been working in the personal development field since 1983. As a counsellor, author, teacher and columnist, she has gained a wide following because of her practical, down-to-earth advice and outgoing personality.

She has written two previous books about stress and writes a weekly advice column for a West Australian newspaper, as well as regular articles for magazines and other publications. Her popular 'Ask Charmaine' segments on ABC Radio and commercial stations are entertaining as well as informative. Her busy schedule includes marketing a series of personal development tapes, operating a mail friendship club and running a counselling practice. She has brought her warmth and humour as well as her vast experience and knowledge to the writing of *Teenage Stress.*

Acknowledgments

I would firstly like to thank Sally Milner, my publisher, without whose support this book may not have been written.

Also, my cat, Max, who kept me company during the many lonely hours in front of the computer.

Fran Head of the Down to Earth bookshop in Perth, who supplied the reading list, and organised a WA launch for the book.

The Citizens' Advice Bureau in Bunbury, WA, who helped me with information about agencies that help adolescents.

Ann Poublon of Dymock's bookshops, WA, who has given me support and encouragement with the marketing of all my books, and who has generously arranged a seminar around this current publication.

No book is a solo effort. I take this opportunity to thank all my colleagues, friends and supporters who have contributed directly and indirectly to the writing of this book and the information contained herein.

Contents

The Nature of Stress 1

Your Home 11

School 24

Sexuality 39

Emotions 60

Health 77

Work and Employment 100

Personal Growth 116

The A to Z of Stress 143

Agencies teenagers can call on 166

Books for teenagers 167

Foreword

One of the main questions I was asked about my last book, *Women and Stress*, was — why is it necessary to write about the stress of only one section of society? Is female stress really different? No doubt the same issue will be raised about *Teenage Stress*. My answer will be the same: the stress itself is essentially the same, but how it manifests and how it is experienced varies according to gender, age, background, personality.

Having worked with teenagers off and on for over twenty years, I have many wonderful memories, stories and insights, some of which I plan to share with you in this book. My main aim is to offer a comprehensive study of teenage stress for the use of young men and women and their parents. The story will unfold via description, anecdotes, case studies and, most importantly, a positive and practical approach to the special challenges of growing up in the 'between' years.

I cannot hope to discuss every teenage issue in detail, and, in order to say anything at all, I have to take the middle road and leave out mention of Aboriginal or migrant teenagers, the handicapped or the brilliant, those with very unusual and specific problems. My premise is that all teenagers share the same feelings, frustrations and fears to some extent, and these cross all boundaries of culture, race, language, intellect and other differences. I hope, therefore, that this book will have something to say to all young people and their families. I, for one, have a deep and genuine love and respect for teenagers, as will be evident through the pages of this book. In many ways, writing this book was a sentimental journey for me as I remembered my own childhood years and all the wonderful classrooms of girls that I knew during my years as a secondary school teacher.

Let us now embark on this journey together, a journey of sharing, discovery and hope. I received some very lovely letters from readers of *Women and Stress*, some from as far away as England. In the hope that the same thing will happen with this book, I include here my postal address for your comments, ideas, questions. I promise to write back to you and help in whatever way I can.

Box 637
Subiaco WA 6008

This book is dedicated to all my students, past and present. Thank you for the joy you brought to my life, the love you left in my heart, and for teaching me much more than I ever taught you.

*Beautiful unlined faces,
like blank pages
waiting to be written upon,
eager young minds
thirsting for knowledge and truth,
healthy bodies
crying out for love.
They call it youth.
I remember it
as the confusion
of living somewhere
between heaven and hell . . .*
NANUSHKA

1 The Nature of Stress

Before anything else, we need to look at the nature of stress itself and how it relates to teenagers in particular. 'Stress' is a word we hear often these days but misconceptions abound as to what it really is. Stress is the external force of pressure that we feel when we're busy, tired or rushed. Sometimes we can cause internal stress in ourselves, but I prefer to make a distinction and call this internal stress 'tension'. So, throughout this book, the terms used are stress for external pressure and tension for internal pressure.

Myths

Many myths surround ideas about stress. Let's take these each in turn, and examine them.

Stress is always a bad or negative thing

Stress is by no means always a negative thing. Athletes and performers of many kinds could not reach the heights of success and glory if they were totally unstressed. We all need an adrenalin rush to give us the impetus to get on with our daily lives, especially when taking exams, going for a job interview, playing sport, taking a driving test, and undertaking similar tasks. Without stress, we would never get up in the mornings. So there *is* such a thing as too little stress! In this book, you will see that if it is harnessed properly, stress can actually be a friend and an ally.

Stress is a modern phenomenon

Stress has been part of human life ever since people first walked the planet. If it appears to be a modern disease, it's only because we talk about it so much more now. Humans have exposed much more of their vulnerability to each other in recent decades, in a whole range of areas. Previously unheard-of topics are now freely aired. Who would have believed, a few years ago, that we would see ads on television selling condoms and tampons, that there would be entire television shows devoted to people airing their dirty linen in public, that stories of incest and rape could be considered prime-time entertainment? Society seems to have a hunger for the more sordid aspects of life, fed by the media, and 'stress' is just an umbrella term for all the harshness, pain and suffering that are part of human existence.

People now exchange stress stories the way they once told each other about their operations. Some actually boast of breakdowns and 'burnout'. One of the things I will be explaining in this book is that it's possible to become a stress junkie, so take all the hype with a grain of salt. It's not clever to go into stress overload, and it *is* avoidable. It's all a matter of balance.

Stress is necessary to 'get the job done'

There is a belief held by a lot of people, especially those who do creative work, that they cannot work except under pressure, so they drive themselves for long hours at a stretch, eat erratically and poorly, hardly sleep and try to overfill their working plates as much as possible. Then, they're surprised when they become too stressed to work or worse still, suffer a severe stress attack.

No, you do not have to be unduly stressed in order to

do good work. You need enough stress to get you motivated, but to work continually under pressure is very wearing on the human body. It breaks down the immune system and makes us more prone to disease. That's why, when people get sick, they'll often say they've been feeling 'run down'.

If you're by nature a stressful person, you can learn to manage your habit

If you are by nature a stressful person, it simply means that you have a particular personality type which is characterised by being an over-achiever, compulsive, a perfectionist, over-anxious, hardworking. This type of personality will almost always be prone to over-do in most areas of life, with habits that attract stress — for instance, taking work home too often, or having a messy desk so that finding every little item is a stress event. I am a recovered stressaholic and can testify to the addictive nature of stress. It's a complex issue that will be explained during the course of this book. The best expert is one who has been through it. Everything I tell you about is based on personal experience. You can change!

Remember, stress is a cause *and* a consequence. It has a circular effect and is very insidious. Its harmful effects accumulate unseen, and that's why prevention is your best weapon against it.

The symptoms of stress

How do you know when you're living with too much stress in your life? I'll discuss the most common symptoms and then relate them specifically to teenagers.

Physical

Physical symptoms include chronic headache, insomnia, tightness in the chest and other parts of the body, chronic fatigue. Tension can be stored in the body and manifest itself as unexplained aches and pains.

Emotional

Emotional reactions to stress can result in relationship breakdown, chronic depression, irritability, mood swings, loss of interest in sex and closeness of all kinds, arguing and quarrelling.

Mental

Stress can cause mental problems such as loss of concentration, poor work performance, loss of memory, difficulty in making decisions, confusion, over-sensitivity.

For teenagers, the same symptoms apply but are usually more extreme. The hormonal changes and developments that rage in the teenage body cause almost constant sensations of stress. Restlessness, grouchiness, erratic moods, crying, depression — these are all everyday companions for the teenager, and must be endured along with the other, already considerable, burdens of growing up.

There is nothing I can say that will minimise the complexity of this time in a person's life. For some teenagers, it's not all bad; for others, every day is a sojourn to the mouth of the volcano. It's no wonder so many want to jump in. There are challenges at every stage of every human life, but I think it's the concentration of problems during teenage which makes it a time most of us shudder to remember. In most cases, the memory is bitter-sweet. We remember acne but also the wonder of our first kiss; feeling ugly and alone but also wonderfully free; the thousand conflicting emotions, the heartbreak of first love, the anger and the ecstasy of being so close to adulthood yet as lost and scared as a child.

Teenage should really be called 'tweenage' because it's like being on a bridge, crossing from one existence to another, yet being forever in limbo, not belonging in either world. If this seems a very dramatic description, it seems so only in recollection, not in the experience, which is more wonderful and more terrifying than words could ever say.

Nothing can ever really diminish these extremes, and perhaps that is as it should be. We each have to cross that bridge and, ultimately, we are alone, but there is one vital weapon that we can take with us: knowledge. With knowledge and awareness, we can feel comforted and brave in the face of adversity — and that's where a book like this one comes in.

Stress and teenagers

With teenagers, it's not a case of identifying stress symptoms, it's more a matter of deciding which ones are the most pronounced. It might even be accurate to say that 'stress' and 'teenage' are synonomous.

What we can judge, however, is the level at which an individual teenager is under stress. This is a very subtle exercise and requires a good deal of practice. Of course, the long-suffering parent is the one who has to decide when the bout of sulking has gone on too long or what the warning signs are when a teenager's depression has become too severe; when to nag, cajole or enquire, and when to say nothing. But history tells us that many, many times, parents misjudge these signs and are faced with the lifelong guilt of a depressed child who commits suicide without, seemingly, any warning; the son or daughter who is discovered to have been taking drugs for years or to be an alcoholic; the pregnant daughter, the violent son. No wonder so many parents despair of the task when their beloved children grow into 'monsters' during that long night between twelve and thirteen.

Parents, when you are about ready to give up, remember that bridge and your child alone upon it — it may help you to endure another unendurable day. If it feels as if you've lost your child, it's because, to a large extent, you have. They are out of your reach for a time. What I aim to do in this book is help you to gain a little more understanding of the teenage psyche, which is, essentially, in constant stress. I can suggest the whys and the hows, why we suffer stress and how to make it better, but unfortunately, I have no magic formula to make all the pain go away. Anyway, who says that would necessarily be a desirable thing? Pain is what keeps us alive and on our toes.

The key is management, making sure the scales tip in our favour so that there's more good stuff than bad stuff in our lives. During the course of this book, I will cheer you with reminders of all the wonderful things that teenagers are: as well as infuriating, maddening, frustrating, impossible, they are also refreshing, honest, straightforward, fascinating and a never-ending source of surprises.

Causes of teenage stress

What causes teenagers to be under too much stress? In brief, the main causes are: the very nature of the teenage years; coping with normal home and family issues; handling authority and what is seen as 'the system'; biological changes and pressures; juggling school, home, sometimes work, and personal pressures; emergence of sexual feelings, dealing with the opposite sex, dating; uncertainty about the future. Plus, all the everyday problems that plague adults as well, such as deadlines, noise, traffic, money problems, work demands.

Home

A difficult family life (and by difficult, I mean unhappy) can have a variety of causes. Even the most tranquil home can be devastated by Typhoon Teenager, so imagine one in which Dad might just have been retrenched, Mum is menopausal, there are financial problems, a bunch of younger children in a too-small house, perhaps problems connected with alcohol or violence — the possibilities, and combinations, are endless. There's no point in expecting a teenager to make concessions to whatever else is going on in the family, because at this point in life, he/she is liable to be totally egocentric and self-absorbed. One of the chief causes of conflict in homes with a teenager is the insistence on the part of a parent that the young person act responsibly and rationally. A reasonable analogy would be someone asking a lion to sit down quietly and eat dinner; that person shouldn't complain if he ends up *being* dinner. It's the nature of the beast.

Boundaries on behaviour can of course be set, but there should be a wide margin given for rebellion and defiance. Being a teenager is hard enough and being the parent of a teenager is hard enough without overly-prescriptive attitudes being brought into play. It's a case of 'less is more'.

So, at home, parental attitudes are crucial when it comes to the amount of stress being generated. Matters such as whether or not the teenager is praised for work well done, loved unconditionally, given the precious gift of time and being listened to, encouraged to learn and take risks in life, given a reasonable amount of responsibility in the home together with large doses of flexibility are vital. Their absence will create tremendous emotional stress which then rebounds on the family as a whole.

Of course, the teenager's own attitude is pivotal to this issue as well. All teenagers have much in common, but some will be more amenable, pleasant, emotional, hardworking, et cetera. than others. While the more placid and the more positive ones might agonise over the same key problems, they may not be as vulnerable to stress simply because of their personalities. But whatever the personality traits, there are many areas of a person's life that can be adapted and improved. That's why stress management techniques are so important.

School

At school, most teenage stress generates from three areas:

peer pressure, problems with study, and conflict with authority figures.

Teenagers encourage each other to smoke, experiment with drugs, drink too much alcohol, give cheek to teachers and thumb their noses at the so-called system. Most go along, and pay the high price for the most desirable commodity in any teenager's life: acceptance. Those on the fringe, for whatever reasons, eventually give up and live the lonely life of not belonging. Young people can be rejected for their looks, their clothes, for being too studious, too quiet, too respectful, and sometimes for no apparent reason at all. Many teenagers who contemplate or commit suicide cite rejection and loneliness as their reason. It's a time when defects stand out, self-esteem is at its lowest ebb and popularity most prized. The stress traps in this arena are numerous and will be looked at in detail in chapter 3.

Problems with learning are a rich source of stressful feelings and pressures. The naturally bright and beautiful have both ends working for them, but most teenagers will either be popular and less academic or studious loners. I don't know of any studies in Australia that have looked at this area of research, perhaps because abstract concepts such as popularity are hard to pin down, but it certainly would unearth some interesting statistics, I'm sure. It's a question of time and energy, and focus — most teenagers have to juggle so many balls in the air that they end up deciding what they're best at and sticking to it. For some, their talent might be simply being the class clown, for others, being good at sport wins acclaim, yet others excel at academic pursuits, and the majority worship at the altar of being one of the gang, of not standing out. Yet, somehow, exams have to be taken, assignments tackled, grades faced up to. There's only so much bluffing and avoiding and getting by that can be done. So schoolwork is a major stress area for teenagers.

And, finally, there are potential problems with teachers, principals and rules. The very nature of a teenager causes him/her to rebel, question, defy. While it's infuriating for adults, it's absolutely essential for young people to go through this stage. In some cases, it's the only time when life is not simply accepted passively, when passions run hot and fear is unknown. Perhaps I need to clarify a point here: on the one hand, teenagers are fearless, on the other, they're petrified. This dilemma sums up a basic challenge for teenagers: their lives are full of contradictions.

When we see a teenager giving cheek to a teacher, all we see is a young person 'being rude'. While the rudeness can never be justified, it often represents a cry for help. Let's face it, teachers are not perfect beings. Some abuse their power, use 'dark sarcasm in the classroom', as the song says, humiliate and belittle their students and are more concerned with their own egos than with teaching. What comeback does a student have after prolonged unfair treatment? Sometimes, young people will explode as stress upon stress piles up; even the most patient and tolerant teenager can 'freak out'. As with adult stress, it doesn't always manifest in the appropriate manner and setting. If teenagers could be rational and mature in dealing with their conflicts, they wouldn't be teenagers. So, frustrations and built-up anger in the classroom may show up days later in the home. I was never rude to the nuns who taught me, despite the various injustices of a typical Catholic convent education, but I was certainly unreasonable and difficult at home at times.

I remember one particular incident when I was about fifteen. A girlfriend and I were not participating in a sports day one Sunday and so arrived in our 'civvies'. Nothing happened until the next morning when we were called out of class to explain our 'bold behaviour'. I was accused of wearing a 'low-cut evening gown', which was in fact a high-necked summer dress! It's funny to look back on now, but when you have to stand at attention and get dressed-down for something you feel you haven't done, it's very humiliating at any age but excruciating for a teenager who has a heightened sense of outrage, especially as it applies to personal pride.

To sum up, teenage stress is caused mainly by:
- The very nature of teenage
- Coping with normal home and family issues
- Handling authority and what is seen as the 'system'
- Biological changes and pressures
- Juggling school, home, sometimes, work and personal pressures
- All the usual things that plague their adult counterparts as well, such as deadlines, noise, traffic, money problems, work demands
- Emergence of sexual feelings, dealing with the opposite sex, dating

Having looked at the issues of stress in a general way, let's move now to the stress management procedures for teenagers and coping techniques for their parents, which I have covered in this book, chapter by chapter.

Write out a list of all the major areas in your everyday life. First, make a list at random, without giving too much thought to reasons or logical sequence. Then, over a period of a month, keep a journal and make a note of the events, places, people and things that you personally find stressful. You will be amazed at what you may discover from such a journey into yourself. Determination and honesty are two prerequisites for this exercise to be effective but the results will make it more than worthwhile. Armed with this new knowledge, you will be able to make meaningful changes.

2 Your Home

What are the most common stresses for you in your home? Are they to do with rebelling against your parents, fighting with your brothers and sisters, not wanting to do things around the house, staying out too much, or all of these things?

Let's look at some everyday issues and challenges that you're likely to experience in your home.

The family unit

When you were a child growing up, you were probably given chores to do, responsibilities that were yours in the home, rules to follow; and, depending if your parents were on the strict side or the soft side, you probably didn't mind. Some of you may come from wealthy homes where cleaners and other helpers do the many tedious tasks of daily housekeeping. Your gender will also perhaps be a factor, as there are still families that expect a boy to do less around the house than a girl. And some of you will resent domestic demands more than others.

If you are by nature tidy, you no doubt keep your own room neat, put things back after you use them and take the rubbish out without being asked. But perhaps you belong to that large percentage of teenagers for whom the home is enemy territory, where every request is interpreted as an invasion of freedom, where your bedroom is a siege area. The posters you have on your walls, the pop music you like to listen to, the outrageous clothes you wear are all part of an overall statement you're making about your beliefs, politics, desires, plans. Then along comes Mum, who says, 'Tidy up your room, it's a pigsty!'. At dinner, Dad starts about the style of your hair and your crumpled clothes and your grades that are just not good enough.

You want to scream, and maybe you do, ruining what should be quality time for the family; maybe you answer back or sit in defiant silence. However you express your anger, it is unlikely to be subtle. A teenager is not mellow or considerate or half-hearted. If you don't like something, you don't pussyfoot around, you just reject. Some of you do it with loud voices, some with silence, but these are just different choices of weapons. It is not comfortable or mellow to be around a teenager, and a home with one of you in it is unlikely to be a peaceful, quiet place. So, before I even begin to examine causes of and solutions for domestic discord, we have to accept that this is a universal problem with only one long-term answer — you turn twenty! In the meantime, there are better ways to cope, and we'll examine some of them in the course of this chapter.

Compromise is, of course, one of the best ways to reduce stress in relationships and create harmony. If you want to go out seven nights a week, and your parents want you to stay home more, why not opt for weekends out and weeknights home or something like that? There is a form of family therapy where parents and teenagers write up an agreement similar to a business contract, covering all aspects of home life. Each point is agreed on by all parties and everyone promises to operate by the terms of the agreement.

This particular form of compromise works very successfully as you can then feel empowered to make decisions in your own life; you don't have to accept blanket rules. But let's face it, boring as the idea might sound, rules are one of life's less pleasant realities. When next you feel like jumping up and down over what you consider to be an outmoded rule, or if you feel you're being prevented from doing the things you like best, think of all the rules and restrictions your parents have to live with. They can't just sleep in or take days off whenever they feel like it; there are road rules and tax rules and work demands and legal impositions and moral belief systems, et cetera. It's all part of living in a society which has to be structured in order to function.

While you're busy demanding respect and attention and justice, ask yourself if you're giving any of those things back. It might be more satisfying to blame and reject but it's a lot less honest. One of the best ways to get along with other people is to use your imagination and 'walk in their shoes' for a while.

Group dynamics work on a system of interplay, sometimes hostile, sometimes co-operative. The personalities of the individuals work either with or against each other. There are bound to be identities in the family group who relate better and those who 'rub each other up the wrong way'. The better you know yourself, the easier it will be to be tolerant and less judgemental of others. You probably think your little brother or sister is the biggest pain ever created and they no doubt think you're 'up yourself', selfish and mean. All you can do is tolerate the members of your family who drive you crazy and seek the company of those who support you and make you feel better about yourself.

Later, you will come to discover that loving and liking are different things. Fate has put you into a particular family group, and it would be inhuman to expect you to like each member equally. But if you can find a way to love them all despite personal differences and preferences, these relationships can last your whole lifetime.

This tolerance is a great lesson for you to learn as it will be a valuable asset in interpersonal relationships later in life. What you can get away with as a teenager will not wash in the adult world, where you are expected to be confident, articulate and accomplished — and that's just to get a hearing, nothing more. You know the old saying, 'the world doesn't owe you a living'. Well, that doesn't only apply to job prospects, salaries and the like; it also means, in an overall sense, that you are responsible for what happens to you, the good things and the bad things. If you make up your mind to that truth early in life, you can save yourself a lot of grief down the track.

Identity crisis

Teenage is the time of the first major identity crisis. You've been through all the developmental stages of childhood, and perhaps you can remember when you first began to realise that you are separate, different, unique. That's when your ego manifested itself in your thinking and behaviour, and you've been testing the waters ever since. So this is, in effect, your first faltering step. This is like learning to walk, in the psychological sense, and is just as exhilarating and scary.

An identity crisis means that you experience doubts about who you are. There are several to come in your lifetime, but none is as vital as this first one. Identity crises are characterised by doubts, fears, rebellion, confusion, mood swings, extreme behaviours. You are constantly in a state of flux — and that's why you can't relax. It's no good we adults saying to you: 'Be yourself', because you don't know what that means yet. Most of us spend our whole lives discovering who we really are.

Let me tell you about false identity and true identity. False identity is based on all the external factors such as your gender, appearance, age, clothes, job. The very moment you came into the world, you were sex-typed, and the process of identification never stops for the rest of your life. Now, while this data about you is necessarily important if you are to live in a complex society, you must never fall into the trap of believing that it *is* you. This is a particularly difficult area for teenagers, because the external factors matter more to you at your age than probably at any other time in life. You are judged every single day on your looks, manner, speech, intelligence, on where you live, what your parents do, your socio-economic level and much, much more.

Keep in mind that these are labels pinned on you for convenience but they only represent a small part of who you really are. The real you is often hidden deep beneath your outer shell, and only the bravest of you will ever let any of it show. If you have parents who encourage you to be true to yourself, to speak up and relate to others in a confident way, you are much more likely to connect with your inner self at an early age. In most families, however, children are still encouraged to be 'seen and not heard'. In extreme cases, they are put down at every opportunity, criticised, ridiculed and told to 'shut up'. A teenager from that type of home will be either severely introverted or very aggressive. The inner self is well and truly masked for fear of hurt and humiliation.

You may be asking yourself as you read: how do I get to know my inner self? At your age, the best way is by having an awareness of the whole identity issue, so that when things happen to you, you can keep them in perspective. Keeping that sense of perspective is extremely difficult for teenagers, but if you can step out of the emotional state for even moments at a time, your life-events will take on a clarity that they couldn't otherwise.

One of the best things I can suggest to help you do this is keeping a daily journal. You probably already do, especially if you are a girl, and you write down what you do each day, your feelings and all the little personal things that you can't even tell your best friend. What I propose is a bit different. The following checklist will help you to get started; later, you can add your own ideas and points.

Identity strategies

> *Monitor the following:*
> - Your intuitions in given situations
> - Your own speech, particularly in anger
> - What other people say to you
> - What other people say about you
> - Your reactions and behaviour in given situations or around certain people. Be aware of flashback emotions, such as taking an instant dislike to someone that you've never met before
> - Your dreams, particularly recurring ones
> - Others' reactions to you
> - Your body language in given situations
> - Tensions within your own body
>
> Keep a journal of thoughts, ideas and feelings as they occur to you, and try to identify any patterns that are obvious.
>
> *Make a list of the following:*
> - Qualities in yourself that you accept and a list of the ones you don't accept
> - Things in your life that make you happy and the things that don't make you happy
> - All of the things you want in life **today**

Conflict

From the time your proud parents first brought you home from the hospital, you have been learning at their hands. Because they are human and imperfect, your parents teach you not only good things but attitudes, ideas, views that you'd be better off not knowing. As a child, you can't distinguish these from the healthy information. You absorb it all holus-bolus. As a teenager, you begin to form views of your own that may be directly opposed to your parents'. This causes a good deal of domestic conflict. It's healthy to hold different views and argue about them as long as it's done in a loving way. Unfortunately, parents often feel threatened by your opposing ideas. They take them as a mark of disrespect, of defiance, so they'll make remarks such as 'How dare you argue with me?' or 'What makes you think you know more than I do?'

Keep in mind that your parents love you and want the best for you **but** they also have a lot of their own ego caught up in who you are and what you achieve. If you appear to fail at the game of life, it's their failure, too, and your triumphs and successes are theirs to share. Some of you may have parents who pushed you to do well from the time you were small, but allowances could be made then for your naughtiness, mischief, rebellion, et cetera. As you enter teenage, the expectations change. This may not be evident at first but, gradually, it will start to manifest in the way your parents speak to you, about you, react to your report cards, structure the rules surrounding your home life, and so on. At the very time when you feel that life has turned into a pressure cooker and you look to your parents to turn down the heat, they seem to be increasingly looking to you to 'do well'. You may feel that nothing you do is good enough.

In my case, the battle was with maths. My mother had been an all-round student, whereas I found maths a total mystery, and lent towards literature, history and languages. It could be argued that it really shouldn't matter what subjects a child is good or poor at in school as long as he/she is trying but, for some reason, Mum couldn't accept my poor maths mark each term. It became the bugbear of my primary school years. One of my strongest childhood memories is praying earnestly in the chapel at the end of every term that Mum would not be too angry about my report. It would be easy to look back with the benefit of hindsight and say that it was cruel of my mother to put such a lot of pressure on a young girl, but her persistence paid off. While I never excelled at maths, I coped sufficiently to take it as a subject right up till my final year at school, and I also learnt the valuable lesson of never giving up simply because something is too hard. I don't own a 'too-hard basket'! I love challenges and pitting myself against a new situation or difficulty.

Keeping the journal I suggested will help you, in similar situations, to see the side benefits of things that hurt you. Let's take a common example: your parents want you to stay home the night before a big test and you are invited to a special concert. They insist, you stay in, sulk and refuse to study; you flunk the test. In your heart, you're glad because you didn't want them to 'win'. At the end of term, you find that you've failed the unit and have to make up the study in the school holidays. Your first inclination might be to rail against your parents for putting you in that situation, but if you stop to think about it, there's a valuable lesson to be gained: we have to live with the consequences of our own actions. None of us has total freedom of choice in life, and we can't party all the time, no matter how much we may want to — or should I say, we can, but there'll be a price to pay. As a teenager, you never seem to stop paying for the things you want, and that's probably because you make a lot of wrong decisions and choices. If you're lucky enough to have parents who let you make those, fine; if you have parents who want to control your actions and restrict your freedom, that's what you've got, so work with it. Remember that the more you fight, the more the rope tightens, so give in where you can and save the fighting for the things that really matter.

Pressure works both ways. When my stepfather died, my teenage brother and sister came to live with me. As I hadn't had children of my own, I was unused to the constant demands they make. My sister leapt on me one day when I arrived home with my arms full of groceries, insisting that I sign a permission slip for a school outing. I asked her if I could do it later as I had my arms full! She persisted and persisted until I lost my temper. I was clearing some room in the freezer and I threw all the frozen meat on to the kitchen floor, shouting, 'None of this is for me! Just give me some breathing space!' A familiar scenario?

Some of you may have to live with more serious and

specific problems such as alcoholic parents or physical abuse. For advice about these matters, see chapter 9.

Main areas of conflict and stress in the home

Let's summarise the main areas of potential conflict and stress for you as a teenager in your home and family life:

- Different personalities and psychologies within the family group
  This is too complex for you to do much about. It is a reality of living with anyone, in any age group. You can only ultimately be yourself and accept that not everyone will like you. The choice you have is simple: should you be someone false who is liked or someone real who will make some friends and some enemies? That's a crossroads we all reach at some point in our lives — it's just a case of sooner or later.
- Clashing of needs, schedules, age-groups
  This is largely a matter of compromise. The clashes usually take the form of small irritations such as one member of the family taking too long in the bathroom when others are waiting, holding up the phone with drawn-out conversations, leaving dishes all over the kitchen after a snack and such-like. The best way to mend these smaller conflicts is by negotiation. Regular family conferences are a great idea and can dispel a lot of ill-feeling. You get the chance to state your views, learn how a democracy works, and help to set your own rules. As I said before, you're much more likely to co-operate if you're given a say in how things run. Suggest this to your family if you don't already do it, and if the idea is not taken up, don't throw in the towel. Your parents may have been brought up in strict autocratic families where parents were the only law.

Try to remember what I said about not hassling over

the petty things. If picking up after yourself or shortening your showers or phone calls is going to lessen the tension around your home, why not do it? Of course, you won't do it if this has become a power game between you and your parents or you and your siblings. As your parents seek to control you, so you'll seek to control your younger brothers or sisters. It's the law of the jungle! If you must rebel over the small things, know you're doing it, at least, and ask yourself why. Understanding often brings surrender, and surrender by choice isn't giving in out of weakness but out of strength.

- Parental expectations

See chapter 2 in the parents' section.

- Stresses and pressures of modern life

It's important to know that you can't separate who you are at home from who you are on the outside. Your personality may change, as is common with teenagers. You may be quiet and sulky at home but the life of the party at school; you may be very well-behaved in class and a 'monster' with your family; confident and relaxed in one setting and a nervous wreck in another. However, when it comes to stress, what you suffer at home, school, friends' places, parties and at work will all be interwoven. If you have a stressful day at school, it is quite likely to affect your home life that night. This aspect of stress you share with adults, for the very simple reason that we are all human beings with nervous systems which react negatively to excess amounts of stress.

So try to be aware of your stress levels on a daily basis. It's important to identify your particular stress areas, the things that pressure you specifically, so that you can limit their presence in your life. For example, if there's a certain activity or person who causes you stress, try to avoid it or them as much as possible. As most teenagers find it difficult to stand up to authority in a positive, assertive way, escape is often the only way out, and teenagers can be very creative at that.

When I was asked to do things I found stressful at school such as sport or debating (it's funny that I'm a professional speaker now!) I would get sick. Of course I see now that it was all psychosomatic, but I actually developed symptoms in order to avoid the stressful situation. I don't recommend this line of action as it only causes stress in a different form. Instead, bite the bullet if you are forced to try something new and do it as well as you can.

Certain people are stressful to us; it's not necessarily their fault, but we don't need to subject ourselves to their company any more than we have to. As a teenager, you are likely to have a lot less choice in this area than adults do; for instance, if you're an average teenager, live at home and attend school, you can hardly get away from your mother or your class teacher or your younger brother, can you? Console yourself with the thought that you're learning one of life's most vital lessons: getting along with people we don't particularly like. There's no escape from this stress at any stage in life but there are ways to limit the negative effects, as we've seen.

We have already looked at some other common stresses of daily life that are likely to plague you; just try to realise that you may be bringing them home with you and don't be too ready to blame your home and family for the way you feel when you arrive back at the end of the day. Yes, your domestic life is quite likely to be imperfect — but no matter how it might appear on the surface, no-one else's is any better, just different. Envy is a waste of energy, an illusion, and it achieves nothing except more stress, and bitterness to boot. So, look at your family members and at your home with the eyes of love and forgive the weaknesses and frailties that you see.

- Power games and disagreements over rules

As we've already discussed, these are likely to be the main area of stress for teenagers. My best advice to you is to accept the existence of rules in your home. Try to see it from your mother's point of view: she has to organise four or five people, not just you. If everyone pleased themselves, chaos would reign. Some of you may live in families where there is no central control. If this is all you've ever known, you no doubt think it's perfectly normal, and I don't mean to make any value judgement about one type of home environment being better than another. However, a family unit is only a small version of society. Neither can function without rules. Imagine the confusion if we didn't have traffic lights or driving speed limits or rules about property ownership and privacy laws! This is discussed more in chapter 9.

In most homes, Mum is the boss, certainly with domestic arrangements such as planning meals, when the washing gets done, who does what chore and so on. She may also go out to a job, as many women do these days, or it could be that you live in a family where Dad stays home and Mum is the breadwinner, or you might live with a single parent. The 'typical' family unit of Mum, Dad and a couple of kids is no longer the norm, but whoever's in charge has an unenviable job so make it easier if you can. If you can't, remember that rebellion is the badge of your age, and that it's okay to be unreasonable and difficult as part of your growing up process — but try to realise why you behave the way you do. When you were small, your parents probably appeared like gods to you, ever loving and giving, even if they weren't like that in reality. By the time you reach teenage, you lose that rosy glow and see your parents with all their imperfections. It is unlikely that you take a very tolerant view of these, as we tend to resent people who have come off their pedestals.

Communication between the generations is still your best weapon, but it is sadly also the most difficult and least-used. Most parents of teenagers say that the worst aspect of the home problems is being treated like the enemy, no longer regarded as kind and loving parents but rather like unfeeling tyrants. (Unfortunately, some parents respond by turning into just that.) If you're a fourteen-year-old girl or a sixteen-year-old boy, you're liable to be at your most stubborn and unpleasant stage. Keep all this in mind as you read on into the following chapters.

In the meantime, keep looking for the signs of love and learn to see them in unlikely places. That favourite cake that your Mum cooks for you, your Dad asking how you're doing in the football team, the silent smile, the encouraging wink, the fact that your parents are available for you, feed, clothe and educate you: these and many other things are unspoken proofs of love. Look for them, and try to overlook the signs of anger and resentment which are often easier to see.

3 School

Not all of you attend school during the whole of your teenage years, but the entire school experience has a profound effect on your life, on the person you are now and will continue to be. The good and bad memories stay with you long after your schooldays are over.

A fellow I was counselling suffered from an unusually high degree of anxiety when it came to dealing with the opposite sex. We finally traced it back to an incident that occurred when he was nine years old. A little girl in his class decided she liked him and wanted to give him a ring. He felt uncomfortable about it and refused it. She then became hysterical, yelling and crying in front of the whole class. My client was mortified and, to this day, has the deepseated fear that if he approaches a woman, she will become demanding and emotional. Hopefully, helping him to remember the cause of his discomfort will lessen his anxiety in the future, but the point of the story is that we all carry unpleasant subconscious memories that still affect us in adult life.

Primary school

You may already have had to deal with a sharp-tongued, impatient teacher or unkind playmates in primary school. I found primary school very stressful, not only because of the maths problem mentioned in chapter 2 but also because I felt alienated, alone, unaccepted. Almost from the first day I entered high school, this changed. I made friends quickly and easily, found schoolwork much easier, and loved going to school each day. This is the reverse of the situation for most young students, who find primary school life relatively peaceful, especially if they attend a local state or church school. Then suddenly they're in high school, and they're nobodies again, having to start from scratch. The work starts piling up, they can't believe how much study they have to do every night, their teachers have much less time to spend with them, and everything seems hard to comprehend.

Tips for learning

My long experience as a teacher led me to the belief that the foundation for good learning has to be laid in primary school. As I'm addressing you now at teenage, there's not much point in worrying about where you might have gone wrong in the past. But if you have learning difficulties now, they ought to be dealt with swiftly and efficiently. If your parents can afford one, a tutor is a good idea, preferably short-term and only for subjects that you have a particular problem with. If this is not an option, then work on your weak areas with the help of a study partner or a teacher who's prepared to give you extra tuition outside the classroom.

It is most important that you don't allow your learning disabilities to escalate because of neglect. Think of the way a snowball gets bigger and bigger as it rolls along and gains momentum — that's what happens when you don't understand something in class and just let it go on. Many adults who are poor spellers or have inadequate writing or numeracy skills can attribute their problems to long-term neglect, and in today's job climate you need to have all the skills available to you.

What can you do apart from asking for help? Those of you in the senior grades have access to computers, library and research facilities, and a lot more freedom to pursue special interests. For example, you get to choose elective units rather than having to study the same subjects across the board. This is a message that you're growing up and are now expected to make decisions that affect your future.

I chose to battle on with maths, and I also took economics, which was a total mystery to me until about six months into Year 11, when I realised my grades were not going to pick up unless I grappled with the concepts and theories that sounded like Greek when they were explained by my teacher. So, every night, I would take one particular theme, say inflation, go through the description in the text book then explain it to myself as if I were the teacher. Slowly but surely, the ideas began to make sense, and with each passing day the lessons became clearer. I eventually found the subject fascinating.

This is a very specific example and my method may not work for all of you, but the trick is to try different things until you find one that's perfect for you. Some of you may benefit from writing out the information you need to remember, or you may like to record the material and play it back over and over; some of you may like to memorise and others will prefer to reason things out in their own minds. There are many successful methods.

Studies indicate that most of you will fall down in the basics such as maths, spelling, writing, reading, comprehension. For all good learning you need comprehension, motivation and organisation. Let's take each of these in turn and look at them more closely.

Comprehension

This is the basis of all learning, if you think about it. If you can't understand, you can't learn. Sure, you can learn blocks of material by rote and reproduce it like a trained parrot, but you will forget all of it within a few days as it was only stored in the short-term memory bank. We've all crammed for exams by this method at some time but it cannot be called 'learning' if little or none is retained. What you truly learn you make your own and can call on at any time. That's why, for many, mechanical, practical skills are much easier to master.

Such things as spelling, vocabulary and maths formulae are best learned by repetition and memorising, but let's take the example of adding words to your personal lexicon. You could learn a list of new words every day and know them perfectly, but unless you use them and practise them in everyday speech, they will remain just collections of letters on a page. I always remember teaching a Year 11 class the word 'lugubrious'. They were absolutely fascinated by the sound and appearance of the word. It became a game to them, and for days afterwards, they went around calling each other and everyone else 'lugubrious', whether it was appropriate or not. The students liked to roll the word around in their mouth and experience it physically. Try it and you'll see what I mean. There are many words you can do that with.

So, comprehension is understanding what lies behind knowledge. This applies to every subject you ever choose to learn. In my opinion, it's better to know a lot about things that interest you than to go through your whole school life just getting by and learning everything superficially. Some of you are probably thinking that my ideas only apply if you're bright to start with. I know many of you may think you're 'dumb'. That's simply not true. Unless you were born with an intellectual disability, which is a different matter, you have an infinite capacity to learn. But first you have to want to learn, and that leads to the next point.

Motivation

Motivation is vital to good learning. Without it, lessons are tedious, information pointless, and school a waste of time. I've always maintained that teachers should be motivators rather than information-providers. This is more true as students move up the grades. If you are given an idea that grabs you, a starting point for research or the thirst for more knowledge on a particular topic, you will never stop learning; but if you're handed the whole story on a platter, that's the end of the experience.

Some of you will no doubt have teachers who make lessons as exciting and interesting as possible for you. But if you don't, don't just give up and say, 'Oh, science is so boring', or 'Old Mrs So-and-So makes French painful'. Find your own strengths and interests and then develop them. Some subjects are never going to grab you, as in my case with maths, but if you're forced to study them, make it a challenge rather than a chore. Concentrate on the things that interest you, because you're always going to do better at tasks that you like, and success breeds success.

So, to the question 'How do I get motivated?', the answer is find your own incentives and reasons for doing things. Other people's dreams and wishes can never work for you. I'm always hearing the familiar cry from teenagers in regard to schoolwork, 'What do I need to learn that for? I'm never going to use it when I leave school.' It's true that many pieces of information you learn at school will simply be forgotten and not used in the future, but I don't believe knowledge is ever wasted. Some of it is simply more relevant to your current life than the rest, but you won't always be sixteen. Later in life, you may call on what you're learning now.

If you know what career path you're interested in pursuing, the best plan is to design your study course around the requirements for that profession or trade. For instance, a teenage client told me recently that she wants to be a vet; because she's not strong in maths, she may ask her parents to let her have short-term tutoring to build up her grades in this area and help her with chemistry, which she'll need later. We'll discuss career preparation further in this chapter. For now, let's look at the need for good organisation, and what that means.

Organisation

Being organised means having a work method and a system that's efficient. You cannot expect to study well and reduce stress if you operate in chaos. The same strategies apply in this as in stress management generally. A lot of stress management is really *time* management. And the same key words apply: balance, relaxation, awareness.

Awareness is the knowledge of what is required to get the job done with the minimum of stress. You know yourself better than anyone else possibly can, so try to identify for yourself your weak areas. In study, for example, you may have difficulty concentrating, or studying for long periods, or remembering details, or keeping your notes in order. Once you establish where you need improvement, you have a workable starting point.

Relaxation requires you to take a quiet and unpressured approach to your tasks and assignments each day. If you allow yourself to get excited, flustered and confused when faced with deadlines or volumes of work or difficult challenges, you can't ever do your best. Study your most successful classmates. I bet they're very focused and calm most of the time. That's not to say you can't have fun or act the goat sometimes, but when you sit down to work, try to reduce distractions so that you have the best chance to absorb the information you require.

Balance involves doing things in the right proportions. There's no point in spending four hours a night doing history homework and neglecting all your other subjects. And you can't do good work if you haven't had enough sleep the night before, or if you eat poorly, or if you never get any exercise and fresh air. These are all unbalanced ways of living, and they're very stressful in the long term.

Successful study is made up of efficient study habits, keeping stress under control, and effective exam techniques. The key to good study is to be organised. Work out the amount of time you have available each week for private study. Divide that time among the number of assignments you have to complete. Allow for research, planning and reading as well as the actual writing.

One of the traps students fall into is going at their assignments without preparation. Balance is once again important. Be sure to allow for periods of leisure, relaxation, meals and sleep. Study should be done in a quiet place, and preferably be uninterrupted. Remove outside stresses and distractions. Set yourself up at the desk/table before you begin writing. Try not to work if you are tired or if it's a very hot day. It would be better to take a nap or wait till the day cools down.

It's best to work in blocks of hours rather than trying to complete a whole assignment in one long stint. That's why it's important to plan ahead. By all means, have regular breaks for stretching and snacks but don't lose your concentration.

Make up a study plan that suits you personally. When you are ready to start working, don't procrastinate as it's much easier once you get started. Positive energy is an important aid so make a fresh start even if you think your study habits have been sloppy up to now. Identify any particular feature of your study programme that you don't think is working well so that you can improve it before it becomes a major flaw.

There are four vulnerable areas you need to watch out for:

Classroom work

The time you spend in the classroom involves a lot more than just listening to your teachers and writing notes or reading. It can make the difference between success and failure, depending on the quality of your attention and interaction. The best teacher I ever had never smiled, never laughed or made a joke, she was barely pleasant and didn't praise or encourage, but she had a marvellous hold over the class, over our minds and our ability to learn. She didn't expect anything but success and that's what she got. Without raising her voice or punishing, she kept us all in line. We would do anything rather than risk her disapproval, not because we liked her but because we respected her totally.

Years later, when I faced a classroom full of students, I found myself adopting a lot of this teacher's methods — except that I also believe in large doses of fun and humour in learning processes. My philosophy of classroom interaction is that a place of learning should be a pleasure to inhabit; there must be accepted rules of behaviour that all parties know and understand; learning should be, as far as possible, undertaken in a spirit of adventure that all share; the atmosphere should be positive and loving; trust and honesty are absolutely vital; each individual student should be encouraged to learn what he/she can. This is where you come in. If you hide at the back of the room, never speak up even if you think you know the answer, day-dream or pass notes or whisper or write shopping lists, nine times out of ten you won't get caught but you'll be cheating yourself. The more actively you participate in class, the better you'll learn.

Remember the point earlier about comprehension? Well, a good aid to comprehension is to practise picking out the key sentence or paragraph when you're listening or reading. Try it the next time you read anything — it becomes second nature after a while, and I have to say it's one of the best skills I learnt at school. It has saved me countless hours over my many years of study since. Concentrate in class and mark off or underline these key points. Always read with a pencil in your hands so that you can doodle little messages to yourself as you go along; for example, a question mark in the margin might mean you're not sure what the author's saying and you want to check it out or read more on the subject or come back to this part of the text later. It's always much more difficult to listen without action — your thoughts start to drift off — so try my suggestion about focusing your attention in this way. You might be surprised how much you learn in a short time, and how much more you enjoy your lessons. Also, risk answering the teachers' questions even if you're not sure you're right, as knowledge often stems from errors. A wise teacher will help you through to the correct answer rather than just saying you're wrong, asking another student or supplying the information.

Of course, classroom dynamics involve more than just learning but we shall come to that a little later in the chapter.

Assignments

The best tip I can offer about these is to keep up with them. That snowball effect I spoke of in regard to poor learning habits applies equally to getting behind with assignments. Try to allot equal time, as far as possible, to all the subjects you have to study for homework or before tests. Map out your work week by week so that you have a rough idea of how you're going to tackle the various requirements of each subject you take. The higher you go up in school, the less guidance you'll get on this, and with freedom comes responsibility.

One of the major causes of stress is feeling overwhelmed by the demands of your schedule, so master your own destiny by being prepared. Having a study partner is very helpful as long as you both put in equal effort. Each of you will have different strengths and it'll be a case of 'two heads are better than one'. But it only works if you're compatible; if you're going to spend precious study time arguing, you may as well battle on alone.

Be clear about what percentage of the total assessment is given to assignment work so that you can designate your study time accordingly. Your grade will largely depend on your performance in weekly essays, projects and, of course, tests.

Exams

As exams approach, check the overview in each of your subjects. Give extra time to your weaker areas. Try not to work yourself up before exam day as tension can prevent you thinking clearly and performing well. Watch your diet on the day before and on the morning of the exam; for example, avoid heavy and strongly spiced foods. Have a good night's sleep; don't let anxiety keep you awake. Never cram just before an exam as it's too late by then and you'll only confuse yourself.

In the exam room, there are also strategies that can help you. Take some deep breaths before you start. Read the paper all the way through without stopping to worry about any particular section. Most exams allow some choice so go back and calmly make your selection. Make brief notes in the margin before you tackle the question as you may run out of steam half way and your jottings will serve as reminders. Answer the questions in the order of your preference so that if you should run out of time at the end, you will have done your best work by then. No matter how little you think you know, tackle every question. An examiner cannot grade a blank page but may be able to find you one or two marks if you have written something.

Match the time you give each question to the allotted marks; for example, 5 marks warrants about a paragraph and 20 marks requires an essay discussion of 2 or 3 pages. There is no point in spending an hour on one question and 10 minutes on another as you won't get any more marks than what the question is worth.

Stay focused. Don't let your mind or your eyes wander. Ideally, allow some time at the end to read back over your work. If you feel panic setting in during the exam, take one or two deep breaths and then continue. Once the exam is over, let go of the experience and practise positive thinking while waiting for the results.

Homework

As with assignments, the important thing is not to get behind. Decide how many hours (realistically) you can spend on homework every night and then allocate time to your various subjects accordingly. I usually recommend that homework is done only after a rest and recreational period, and preferably after the evening meal. After school ends for the day, outdoor activities are best to clear the mind, followed by some relaxation and nourishing food. Then homework can be tackled productively.

Homework goals should be set according to priority; for example, do the work due in the next day first but also set aside some general study and review time, if possible. If you have a big assignment that you've been given two or three weeks to complete, do a bit each night, even if it's only reading so that you don't end up with a massive job and two days to hand it in! If your teacher gave you several weeks, it stands to reason that's how long the job takes.

These are mainly common-sense suggestions, but no doubt most of you don't operate by these rules. You probably blunder along doing your schoolwork piecemeal and wondering why you're exhausted, in a muddle and stressed-out most of the time. Now you know and you have a choice.

More study tips

If a poor memory is your problem, here's a simple tip. Good memory is basically made up of two components: interest and concentration. Things you're interested in, you're more inclined to remember. Take the case of being introduced at a party. The names you'll tend to recall after the introductions have been made are those that belong to the people you expect to talk to further. Therefore, you concentrated when their names were said to you and you remembered them. That's why vague people have the worst memories: their minds are always on something else.

One way to sharpen your memory is to practise relying on it rather than writing everything down. If you have a long list of shopping or dates or details to retain, try the association game that works particularly well for me. Here's how it goes: you have to go to the supermarket and you need milk, tissues, toilet paper and ink, so all you have to do is think of the word 'mitt' and each letter will remind you of one thing on your list. That's an easy one as it actually forms a word, but letters that form very familiar initials like ABC or BBC or IBM are also easy to remember. You get the point, anyway. Keep practising and it will come automatically after a while.

Pressures

We can't leave this section on school without examining some of the more general pressures that cause teenagers stress.

Peer group pressure

You've all heard this expression and have experienced it in one form or another. It's neither good nor bad, it just exists, and is not unique to the teenage years. In simple terms, it means the influence of the people who are in our age-group and deal with us directly on a day-to-day basis. They will tend to have an opinion about everything we do and their approval is very desirable to us. If this is allowed to disempower us to the extent that we no longer think for ourselves and blindly follow the majority then it's a problem. For teenagers, the danger is that you are very impressionable and care a lot about your peers' approval. You are constantly experimenting and may be talked into trying things you would normally leave alone, such as smoking, alcohol, drugs, speeding in cars, stealing, vandalising.

The nature of the teenager is to push limits and break down barriers, to try new things and take chances. That in itself is fine, but I would like to see you choose your own dragons to slay and your own dreams to pursue, not be used as a pawn in the games of so-called friends. So, just keep that in mind the next time you're asked to do something you know is wrong or that you simply don't wish to do. Don't fall for the emotional blackmail behind such comments as 'If you were my friend, you'd come along.'

A common and dangerous form of peer group pressure has to do with dating and sexual experimentation (see chapter 4). Boys, watch out for the old trap of your mates bragging that they have had sex and teasing you for being 'slow'. Girls, don't fall for the 'If you loved me, you'd have sex with me' line. Sex is far too wonderful and important to rush into at someone else's pace.

Anxiety about the future

One of the greatest pressures you face during your school years is the anxiety over your future plans and success. There are parental and society's expectations, the necessity for good grades, job prospects, decisions about careers, and the current economic conditions. When I was at school, we decided what we wanted to do with our lives and we just went out and did it. The reality for today's teenagers is a lot more complicated. You face a great deal more competition and have obstacles to overcome that earlier generations were free of.

One obvious example is the high incidence of unemployment. Your grandparents went through wars and the Depression, but no matter how terrible these things were, they were short-lived. Unemployment in Australia today is a chronic problem. Some of you will join the dole queues to become further statistics in the system. If I could wave a magic wand to ensure satisfying, well-paid work for all of you, I would do it. But, of course, I can only speak in a general way to those of you who don't want to live on benefits and waste whatever abilities you have. You've probably heard from every source, from teachers to parents to religious advisers, about the importance of 'making something of yourself'. If you follow the practical ideas laid out for you in this book, you will have a blueprint for success, not just a vague wish. You have enough real pressure in your lives without the stress of finding all the answers by yourself. And the mistakes you make? Well, they're just par for the course.

Classroom pressure

The main causes of this are boredom, not being able to answer the teacher's questions, conflict with other students, and misbehaving. You feel bored when you can't follow the lesson or because your mind is wandering. Human concentration wanes every seven minutes, so it's not just you. Try to keep focused. You may be amazed at how much more you'll remember from your classes if you pay attention.

If you're constantly in a state of anxiety over the possibility of being asked a question, it's probably because you aren't listening well or you don't understand the material. You needn't be afraid to answer wrongly as most teachers would prefer to find out what you don't know. That's what classroom lessons are all about. Homework is the time for quiet, private work, and we have exams and tests to find out what you have learned, but the classroom is your place to enquire and learn and make mistakes. Use it.

The classroom is a microcosm, a small world of its own, so there will be the same potential for conflicts and other human emotions there as anywhere else. The main difference is that it is also a controlled environment. The teacher has to maintain control and discipline in order to get any work done. So conflicts, rather than being openly hostile, are likely to seethe below the surface. When the teacher's back is turned, one student may thump another or do something to get someone else into trouble. The teacher, too, suffers tension and frustration because of students who continually disrupt classes, too much noise and/or talking, kids who don't want to learn and prevent their classmates from getting their work done, and many other small and big irritations. Effective teachers are patient but they're also human; remember that the next time you think it's amusing to taunt them, give cheek or disturb the peace of the class.

Misbehaving is directly related to the last point, and can range from passing notes to running around and screaming. A student of mine years ago used to disrupt every class by jumping up and down from her seat, talking loudly, cracking weak jokes and laughing, stirring the other students, asking inane questions. It got so that no teacher would have her in the class and she spent most of the day studying by herself in the secretary's office. When I spoke to her alone, she was perfectly reasonable and I couldn't understand her compulsive need to misbehave in class until I looked into her family history. Her father was a famous doctor, her mother a socialite, her sister a rare beauty, and there was she — lumpy, ungainly, spotty, fat and very, very plain. This was the classic second child syndrome in spades! The girl's behaviour demonstrated a greater than usual hunger for attention. She was asking for it in the only way she knew how as she felt incapable of getting it in the normal way and was being bypassed in the family circle.

This is an extreme case, yet teenagers misbehave in class every day of the week. Those who don't are branded 'goody-goodys'. If you are one of those who do, think about why you do it and whether it relates to any of the above three points. You could also be releasing some of the stress from other areas of your life, for example, if you have a situation at home that's bothering you, you may not be able to express the frustration and anger there so you talk in class or abuse the teacher or hit your classmates. Try to come to grips with this and see your school counsellor for further help.

So, to summarise: plan your work, be as organised as possible, follow your own principles but seek advice and help where necessary, give every area of your life its due measure, reduce your stress levels by being calm and relaxed, and **have fun**. All you can do is your best, and worrying never helped anyone.

4 Sexuality

One of the greatest stresses you are likely to encounter is in the sexual area. As a teenager, you are mainly stressed because you live in a twilight world of confusion and mixed emotions. You are continually told that you are no longer a child and should act responsibly, but, on the other hand, parents often set arbitrary standards of behaviour which restrict and frustrate teenagers. One of the most common complaints I hear from young men and women is 'I'm told to grow up but, every time I try to do something that I want to do, I get into trouble.'

Nowhere is this conflict more pronounced than in matters of sexual feelings and expression. In this chapter, we will look at the controversial subject of sex education, and discuss the difficulties of budding sexual awareness, dating and sexual activity.

Sex education

Even in the enlightened 90s, the issue of sex education and whose responsibility it should be is not clearly defined. The community remains divided on whether children and young people should be taught the 'facts of life' by parents or teachers, or be left to find out for themselves from peers and books. Let's look at the pros and cons of each alternative, starting with the last one.

Sex education at random

Most experts affirm that children need some kind of adult guidance when learning about sex. Ideally, you should be told the most important details of intercourse, conception, pregnancy and birth before the onset of puberty. My mother took me aside when I was about ten and explained about menstruation, and how men and women love each other and make babies. I recall that I wasn't very interested at the time but, as my periods began early (at eleven), Mum's timing was perfect. There was none of the fear or revulsion associated with the onset of bleeding that Mum herself had experienced because she was totally ignorant of the facts at the time. I simply announced to her one day when she came home from work, 'You know that thing you told me about? It happened today.' I would wish this natural approach for every child.

Unfortunately, some parents are not comfortable with their own sexuality and are therefore reluctant or unable to play a teaching role with their children. If you are in this category and there's no formal sex education taught at your school, you are left to flounder until circumstances bring you into contact with the information.

Most of you know the basic facts by the time you enter high school, and you would have an awareness of your own sexual identity by then. But who teaches you about caring and self-respect and contraception if you pick up your knowledge from snippets of locker-room anecdotes and playground gossip? There's no way to prevent you picking up incidental information these days. You only have to turn on the TV to hear frank discussion of condoms, tampons and intercourse. In some ways, this is a positive thing — it certainly has ensured that sex as a subject can no longer stay locked in the cupboard of ignorance.

It's obvious from what I've said so far that I favour

formalised sex education. But who should do it, the parents or the school?

Sex education in the home

Those of you who enter high school without at least a rudimentary knowledge of sex are disadvantaged in two ways: you'll be behind those students who have been tutored at home, and you'll be ill-equipped to deal with real-life sexual pressures such as whether or not to have intercourse before you feel ready. I'm not suggesting that everyone who learns about sex incidentally will grow up with a distorted or unhealthy attitude, but statistics show that those of you who come from homes in which sex is not freely discussed may experience difficulties in relationships and normal sexual enjoyment later on in life. I'm sure your parents would prefer that you learn about sex in the home or classroom, rather than in the pages of pornographic literature or the back seat of a car.

So, how do you get them to talk about sex if they're reluctant to, without it becoming an embarrassment or a source of conflict? Questions are best. It's much easier for your Mum or Dad to give you information on a specific matter than if you just ask them to tell you about sex or love-making in general. Don't press if they only give you a scanty answer as you can always ask again, but if you pressure them you might turn them right off and cause them to clam up the next time.

Be tolerant of your parents' feelings. They may not mean to be evasive but perhaps are just very private about this area of life. They can only offer you what they know themselves from their upbringing and experience. It's no use accusing them of being old-fashioned or behind the times as your parents grew up in a different world, one in which sex was not discussed by 'nice' people in mixed company, and certainly not in public and in the media. The generation gap is never more pronounced than in the area of sexual matters. Keep that in mind and tread lightly.

If you really can't get a discussion going at home, you may have an aunt or uncle or neighbour with whom you feel more comfortable, and that person might be a better choice of information-giver for you.

Sex education at school

Even in cases where parents do assume responsibility for sex education, it's still desirable for schools to offer a programme, particularly for senior high school classes. If sex is not discussed openly at school at all, you are not given the opportunity to voice opinions or express areas of concern in an open forum. It's to be expected that you'll be embarrassed to start with or send the whole thing up, but once these initial barriers are removed, a worthwhile exchange can ensue, given the right instructor. There's no point having a teacher who's uncomfortable with the subject or one with strong moral views about sexual behaviour. You need facts, together with impartial guidance. If we want you to be responsible, we need to supply you with the tools, and intelligent sex education is one of those tools.

An ideal school programme will be organised something like this:

- It should begin in the late primary years, but increase from Year 10 onwards.
- It should be conducted in small, co-ed classes, unless it's a one-sex school.
- It should involve the same group of students over a period so that shyness and embarrassment can gradually be overcome.
- It should incorporate some formal instruction with such things as diagrams, statistics, charts included.
- The bulk of classtime should be given over to free discussion and questions.
- It should be informative without being stuffy. If students giggle over pictures of genitalia, for instance, they shouldn't

be reprimanded as humour can be an effective as an aid in teaching.
- It should be conducted by a teacher sympathetic to the delicate nature of the subject and prepared to encourage questions and ideas.

When I went to school, there was certainly no question of sex education in primary school. In fact, sex was very much a taboo subject. Diagrams of the human body in our biology texts were pasted up so that those pages wouldn't open, and at film screenings, the good sisters would blacken the screen if any kissing, no matter how chaste, came on. The only sex instruction I recall was in our school-leaving year. By then, my schoolchums and I thought we were pretty knowledgeable and so we simply made fun of the efforts of the unfortunate local priest who had been asked to come in and teach us about sex. Deliberately provocative offerings would be placed in the question box, such as 'At what age should a girl wear a bra?' and 'Is it a mortal sin to French kiss?' What horrors we were!

But the point is that there was no correlation between what was going on in our lives and the mumblings of our unsuitable tutor. There we were, seventeen years old, most of us dating, experimenting to various degrees, bursting with all the natural longings of our age, more eager to learn about life in between the covers of a bed than a book — official sex education had come too late for us. The answers offered to our questions were so remote from reality that they just cracked us up rather than address any relevant issues. For instance, a girl asked, 'How long should a kiss last?' and the priest answered, 'Only as long as it takes to say the Lord's Prayer'!

Most of you have a favourite teacher, one to whom you can talk freely. In the absence of a sex education programme as such, you may prefer to see a particular teacher privately to ask for information or advice. There are so many potential traps for you at this stage of your development: what to do about sexual urges, whether or not to have intercourse with a boy/girlfriend, what type of contraceptive is best, how to deal with feelings of guilt and anxiety, and many, many more. A well-placed conversation with a trusted adult can make the difference between despair and mature decision-making.

In certain school subjects, such as biology and literature, sex often comes up in an incidental discussion, and that's a way for sex to form part of the curriculum without a formal approach. Nearly every novel has some romance or love component, and this can lead naturally to a discussion of sexual behaviour in the context of the book which also relates to real life.

Sex is an activity that most of us conduct throughout our lives. It is a beautiful and natural part of life and we want to teach you that. This needs to be handled carefully. By the time you get to Year 10 or 11 at school, you are pretty resistant to your family's ideas, values and rules. That's another reason why sex education at home needs to take place much earlier. At age sixteen or seventeen, you will talk about sex at school, to friends and possibly to a teacher, but only in rare cases to a parent.

If your school doesn't offer any kind of sex education programme at all, ask your class teacher about it as there are specialist sex educators who go out to schools and talk about the health aspects as well as sexual attitudes and behaviour.

If all else fails, check out the library for up-to-date literature on this topic. You may not need the biological facts but sex is a very complex human activity, and remember knowledge is power: the more you know, the easier your path through life will be. Of course, some things you can never learn except by experiencing them first-hand, but a good foundation will ensure that you are not making decisions blindly or for the wrong reasons.

No doubt you are discussing sex amongst yourselves, and that's healthy — to a point. What was said in chapter 3 about peer pressure could come into play in this area. You need informed talk and exchange, and you also need to talk freely with your own peers about your doubts and ideas and uncertainties. You are living in a much more permissive age than any other generation before you. This brings disadvantages as well as advantages. 'Familiarity breeds contempt' they say, and it would be tragic if you thought of sex as ordinary or even tawdry because it's cheapened and dehumanised by constant exposure.

Puberty

Most adults look back on puberty as being one of the most frustrating, difficult times of their lives. It's not hard to see why. Life holds out nothing but promise, yet reality is often painful and embarrassing. From my personal and professional experience, the worst time for girls is around fourteen or fifteen years of age, and for boys about seventeen or eighteen. Girls reach sexual maturity before boys, and it follows that they also arrive earlier at their most difficult and moody stage.

Boys

The difficulties for boys at puberty are more overt, as your sexual urges manifest for the first time. 'Wet dreams' can occur before this time but are largely involuntary. Active and enthusiastic masturbation usually begins at puberty, as sexual tension accelerates. If regular masturbation occurs too long before puberty, it can lead to premature ejaculation in later life, as patterns of self-satisfaction are established between onset of masturbation and first intercourse. At this time, you find it difficult to keep your mind on anything but sex, and it is not uncommon for you to masturbate several times a day. This intense desire usually lasts for one or two years, and it's important not to feel guilty about it. If your parents are people with strong religious convictions, they may believe that this behaviour is morally wrong, so if you're found masturbating, you might get yelled at or ridiculed, but the whole thing will blow over with time. As you develop, your urges will tone down and other issues will take precedence. Guilt is very destructive, so try not to dwell on negative feelings about your sexual urges and desires.

Case study. Barry, a patient of mine, was addicted to antisocial behaviour. He was happily married with a young family but couldn't stop himself being a peeping tom. From time to time, when the urge became too strong, he would hide in the bushes in front of a block of flats and look at women undressing in their bedrooms. While I was counselling him he was caught in the act of 'perving', and this provided the jolt he needed. Working with me through his past, he came to realise that his need to get sexually aroused by looking at women in this furtive way was masking the need to be caught. It was actually the secretive nature of his actions that gave him a sexual thrill. We traced it back to a memory he had of reading 'dirty' books in the laneway behind his house. A neighbour would throw out a boxful and Barry liked to look at them and masturbate at the same time. This pattern of sexual thrill/guilt stayed with him long after the behaviour stopped, and his adult mind sought to recapture those feelings of excitement by finding another way to create them.

Girls

For girls, the effects of puberty are felt most acutely in physical and hormonal changes. Budding breasts and the onset of menstruation are key manifestations and can cause varying degrees of discomfort. Some of you develop seemingly without struggle while others suffer every inch of the way. Mood swings are also part of the process and you can be obnoxious and unpredictable, as any parent of a teenage girl will confirm. Sexual tension can be expected and you too may masturbate regularly to relieve tension.

Homosexuality

Homosexual experiences are possible for both sexes, whether or not they are a forerunner to adult sexual preferences.

These are often due to the intensity of feelings in females and competitiveness in males.

We will see in chapter 5 how important friendship is to the teenage girl. It is the most influential factor in your life. You would rather almost anything than the loss of status with your peers, and this can go to extreme lengths: health, schoolwork, future, family are all minor considerations by comparison. If these relationships are threatened in any way, they can take on sexual undertones and even specific behaviours. Sometimes, kissing and touching begin as expressions of closeness and then develop into more. Or two teenage girls may experiment in bed together for fun, or they may make love in a spirit of defiance when the world of authority gets too oppressive.

I recall a student of mine at a boarding school coming to me in tears because she and a girlfriend had been showering together as they were late for tea; they were 'caught' by a housemother who proceeded to call them names and tell them they were 'dirty little girls' for being together in the shower. This is a bit like my being accused of wearing a 'low-cut evening gown', but a lot more serious. Don't let this type of injustice push you into doing things you may not really want to do. The only consolation I can offer is that you will laugh about it in years to come — unless, of course, you allow small minds to damage your self-esteem, which is a delicate matter for a teenager at the best of times.

With boys, it is the sexual nature of the male that can cause homosexual behaviour. Proximity in toilets, bathrooms, locker-rooms and playing fields can cause involuntary erection, which can then easily lead to mutual masturbation, voyeurism or sexual fondling. Sex games are usually generated in a spirit of bravado, such as measuring each other's penises to see who can boast the larger one, or peeing from a distance to see whose aim is the best, or even group masturbation to see who can ejaculate first. This is largely harmless and short-lived, and should only be a matter of concern if the experiments are dangerous in any way or if boys are being forced into games they're not ready for. Adult supervision isn't possible all the time, but do not hesitate to complain if you're being forced into any such activities against your will. This is too serious to endure out of misguided loyalty or hero worship or even fear.

Of course, it's a totally different situation for those of you who experience genuinely homosexual desires. 'Coming out' is difficult enough for adult gays but can be an excruciating decision for teenagers. Many of you choose to say nothing, but for the girl who's very 'butch' in appearance and for the effeminate guy, there may be little choice. There are gay counselling services and teenage phone lines for young people who are caught in this physical and emotional crisis. Most of you fear your parents finding out and the ridicule of your peers. Sexual activity for you is quite likely to be non-existent due to the overpowering fear of discovery and rejection.

Teenage gays are under tremendous stress as you form a sub-culture not easily tolerated by mainstream teenagers. In rare cases, those of you who believe you are gay are brave and mature enough to go out socially to meet other gays. But most of you have nowhere to go with your sexual feelings and you live constantly in fear and anxiety. You have all the same doubts and inadequacies as other teenagers and much less information. Most parents are ill-informed about the whole gay issue and would almost prefer to hear that their child is dying than homosexual.

Some of the cases I have worked with include a girl who was very confused and frightened by her homosexual feelings, saw a school counsellor and was told, 'You'll just have to accept it.' Another girl was so afraid of her European family finding out that she planned to move interstate as soon as she left university.

As with all teenage problems, they are short-lived in so far as you find them easier to deal with when you move into the later stages of the teenage years. Those you take into adult life are the more complex ones which plague us all.

If you are committed to homosexuality as a way of life, find out as much as you can about it now before you take any active steps. Experimentation is normal and most teenagers, male and female, will have some kind of homosexual experience during puberty. If this has happened to you or you're inclined to try it, don't feel ashamed. It doesn't make you 'bad' and it doesn't mean you're necessarily gay. It just means that you have feelings which you want to try out. This is an ongoing situation during the teenage years, in all areas.

Changes

Puberty is not only a time of sexual awakening for boys and girls; it is a time of discovery in many areas and involves physical changes, and changes in feelings and attitudes. You literally watch yourselves change on a daily basis. A clear face one day is a mass of pimples the next; today's best friend is a detested enemy tomorrow; likes and dislikes alternate constantly, and body shape is a matter of interminable concern. Boys and girls start noticing each other in a different way, and that causes a thousand new anxieties. The problem is that while desire is strong, you possess none of the social skills needed to turn aspirations into reality.

Girls are, on the whole, more self-confident, but even in the 90s, you still tend to wait around for boys to ask you out. You spend a great deal of time fussing with your appearance but are nevertheless quite sure that you have the world's knobbiest knees or the largest nose or the stringiest hair. The whole business of sexual attraction is torturous for teenagers. And once you get to dating age, usually around fifteen or sixteen, new pressures emerge.

Dating

Young love

We've seen how lonely and frightening the world can be for the teenager and what a large role peers and friends play.

It's not hard to see how influential a boyfriend or girlfriend can be. Suddenly, when you have a special friend you are no longer living in an alien environment where no-one understands your problems, pressures and needs. You tend to cling to and make idols of each other in a way that is unique to the teenage psyche. This love is absolute. Often, all other aspects of everyday life are blurred into the shadows as couples dreamily gaze at each other and contemplate a rosy future. There are few people who have not experienced young love, or can forget its bitter-sweet taste.

The danger is in the intensity which defies all reason and restriction. More family quarrels are caused by this issue than almost any other (see chapter 5). You are not going to like it if your parents try to prevent you seeing a particular friend or going out in a group or liking someone. Because your friends are paramount in your life at this time, you are inclined to be very protective and defensive about any criticism, even if, in your heart, you know your parents are right. You come under your parents' authority so you do have to obey them in some things even if you violently disagree. This, too, is part of the pain of young adulthood, but remember, your parents are always on your side, no matter how it might appear. I am a great believer in allowing people to learn by their own mistakes, but some of your parents will take the view that their opinions and their insistence on the rules are totally justified and there's no room for discussion.

The intensity of your feelings can also lead to recklessness and carelessness, evidenced by such behaviours as running away together, indulging in sex before either party is ready, not being prepared in regard to contraception, not taking health precautions, unwanted pregnancies, early marriage, dropping out of school prematurely, abortion — the list is endless.

This is why sex education is so crucial in the pre-puberty or immediately post-puberty stage of development so that choices are made with full knowledge. That's not to say that those of you who are well taught won't make the same mistakes as your more ignorant counterparts, but at least you are aware of the alternatives.

Family planning clinics and teenage pregnancy centres have sprung up in the community in direct response to the increasing need for practical help and support. Teenage girls continue to fall pregnant at an alarming rate: you fall in love and fall pregnant in the 90s just as teenage girls did in the 20s and 40s and 60s. There is no magic solution. What is needed is more and more understanding of what makes you tick.

Most of the social problems that beset young people can be traced back to loneliness, a lack of family love and low self-esteem. When teenage girls fall pregnant today, you're still faced with the same dilemmas: How do you tell your parents? Should you have an abortion? If you keep the baby, will you be able to cope? What other choices are there? This is decision-making at its most crucial, as the baby's life and well-being as well as your future all hang in the balance. Being an unmarried mother is not as shameful as it used to be in society's eyes, but pregnant girls still have to deal with censure and ridicule from parents, friends, neighbours, teachers.

Then there are all the practical considerations. Long after the decision is made, the consequences live on. I've had letters from women who gave up their babies as teenage mothers and now, twenty or thirty years after the event, still live with guilt and regret. It's easy for me to tell them that these are wasted emotions but the powerful pain of giving up a baby to adoptive parents or having a foetus aborted never seems to diminish.

It is outside the scope of this book to discuss in detail abortion and adoption procedures and the moral arguments that continue to rage for and against them. I believe you should be counselled on all your options so that, with loving guidance, you can make informed decisions. I think it's wrong for you to be pressured into one action or another by adult standards and moral positions.

The dating game

Dating is not always about true love. It is an excruciating business for many teenagers due to shyness, an inability to speak out, self-consciousness over body shape or size, acne or stuttering, and a deep-seated fear of being rejected. That's a heavy load for any age-group to carry, and you already have more hang-ups than you can reasonably be expected to deal with. Your isolation means that you feel unable to talk about your fears and uncertainties with anyone apart from trusted close friends. Then there are those of you who can't seem to make friends at all, let alone date.

Take away the teenagers who find first love and start going steady almost immediately and those who can't get to first base, and what are you left with? The vast majority of kids between fourteen and seventeen who are at school and get asked out on dates on a regular basis. Boys still have to do most of the asking, but sometimes girls have to get partners for school dances and such-like and have to take the initiative. Some parents are more strict than others about rules for dating, such as what age it should start, what time girls have to be home, and how many nights out are allowed in a week.

The laws of etiquette have certainly relaxed; for example, the days of boys having to meet parents before going out are well and truly over. When I was teaching teenage girls, I counselled them to insist on at least basic good manners from their partners, such as that they come to the door to pick them up and not just yell or beep their car horns! The standard reply to this suggestion was, 'But the boy might not ask me out again if I insist that he does that.' It comes back to self-respect and insisting on being treated well, I told my students.

There are a whole range of behaviours which relate to dating, and most relate to self-respect and concern for others. If you are not taught to be considerate, you will grow into the kind of adult who breaks appointments at the last minute, fails to show up for arrangements, and asks people out at very short notice. Low self-esteem manifests in such behaviours as always being available, no matter how badly a partner behaves, feeling privileged to be asked out, even when a date is not desirable, and accepting bad manners when being taken out.

My students used to ask me questions such as how to avoid a goodnight kiss if it's not wanted, how to let a boy down gently if a second date is not on the cards, how to let a boy know he's liked, and how to get him to ask for a date if he's a bit slow on the uptake. Many of the answers to these questions are supplied in chapter 5, but for now, just let me say that most delicate situations are best handled with good humour and kindness. For example, it's far kinder to say goodnight to a boy in the car, in a friendly and pleasant way, than to let him see you to the door and put him through the excruciating business of 'trying it on', only to be refused. Here are some simple suggestions which may sound funny but do work.

- Have your hand on the car door handle a bit before you arrive at your destination so that you can jump out quickly without it looking awkward.
- Give your date a quick peck on the cheek before he/she has time to react. The element of surprise works every time.
- Let your date take you to the front door, step inside, shut the flyscreen door behind you and remain there talking for a while.

Sexual activity

Sexual activity for teenagers can range from holding hands to full intercourse. Very often, it's a case of 'the blind leading the blind', as both parties are raw recruits at the game of loving. Even very young men can experience impotence brought on by fear and anxiety. The youngest patient I ever counselled for this condition was eighteen, but I daresay it can happen earlier and go unrecognised. The boy I saw had been badly embarrassed by a girl when he was younger. In mixed company, she laughed at the size of his penis when he stepped out of the shower. Needless to say, he remembered this every time he attempted to make love thereafter.

Impotence, however, is not the most prevalent problem for your age-group. There are all the issues I mentioned earlier such as ignorance about contraception, fear of being found out, parental censure, and lack of opportunity, just to name the obvious ones. When I was a teenager, we had a standing joke that when we parked and 'had a grope', we didn't know what we were groping for! It was a more innocent time when sexual intercourse was not common for well-brought-up boys and girls. Sure, we wanted to and eventually did 'everything but', yet it was always clearly understood that certain limits were not to be exceeded. Girls who went 'all the way' and/or got pregnant were 'cheap' and 'bad'. Of course, no such judgements were made about the boys they had sex with — the double standard was alive and well in those days, and, unfortunately, is still thriving in many areas of life today.

There's a lot more pressure on young people today to try everything, sex being one of the lesser evils in many cases. Statistically, girls are still having sex for the first time at approximately sixteen or seventeen, and boys at fourteen or fifteen. Many start earlier, and I have heard of cases where men are still virgins in their fifties or remain celibate into their twenties or thirties. As always, the exceptions prove the rule.

Certainly, there's a lot more public education today because of the existence of AIDS. Condoms may have been in boys' pockets in my day but no decent girl would ever carry or provide one, and if the subject of 'french letters' ever arose, it was whispered like a dirty joke. Now, they're freely available and you are taught and encouraged to use them, for health reasons. However, please don't feel you have to rush into sexual activity just because you can now practise 'safe sex'. Sex is still more than just a physical experience.

Preventing AIDS and pregnancy isn't all you have to worry about. Throughout your life, you will be called upon to make enlightened decisions about your body and your relationships. The teenage years are a great time to start learning to do that. There are endless documentaries and surveys trying to find out if, in fact, teenagers are having less sex in the 90s because of health fears and all the warnings over promiscuous behaviour. My view is that for teenagers, the need to experiment and the need to express emotional energy are driving forces, so, regardless of anything the adult world says, you're going to test the waters yourself, even if you put yourself at risk. As a general guide, one could say that girls will tend to play down the role of sex in interactions with boys while boys will tend to exaggerate it when dealing with girls.

I was given a lot of freedom as a teenager but I remember my mother didn't like my parking in the driveway after dates. Sometimes, my boyfriends and I would 'neck' out there for an hour or so and Mum was concerned about what the neighbours would think. My answer was that I was a lot less likely to get up to much in the car in front of the house than if we'd parked down at the river or in some park. I have many funny memories of dates that went wrong. One that always comes to mind is having a slap and tickle in a caravan parked in the front yard of my boyfriend's home. Suddenly, the light on the front porch snapped on and the guy's mother came out, saw the movement in the caravan, guessed what was going on and called out, 'Take that girl home right now!' It was all fairly harmless in those days — no AIDS, condoms or intercourse, just lots of groping and good old Catholic guilt!

Just be sure why you do things and respect yourself in all you do. If you live by that principle, you can't go far wrong. You have loving parents, teachers and friends to guide you and to support you if you make a mistake. Some of you may be true 'loners' and lack this support structure, but you always have your own integrity. There is more about your inner voice in chapter 8.

I speak of the powerlessness of children in my book *Women and Stress,* and this applies equally to teenagers. It isn't all gloom and doom. There is a lot about teenage life that can be joyful and uplifting, as we've seen in earlier chapters. But I think sexual activity is unlikely to be one of the happy areas.

The first time

Just kissing can be either torturous or exhilarating to a teenager. Some of you probably practise the art by the hour, using the back of the hand, a cushion or the bathroom mirror as a lips-substitute. There is nothing sexual about this exercise — it is serious business! You don't want it going around that you're a bad kisser! Reputations are made or broken by gossip and innuendo on the school grapevine. The question 'Are you getting any?' is an extension of the pubescent horseplay discussed earlier in this chapter. Although the question stems largely from bravado, there certainly is genuine curiosity and the boy who can answer yes becomes an instant hero to his mates. For a girl, an affirmative answer raises her high in her friends' estimation: up go the cries 'How brave', 'How exciting', 'What was it like?'

But what is the first time really like? Pretty terrible by most accounts. The Peggy Lee song 'Is that all there is?' springs to mind. Both males and females questioned on this subject complain that their first experience of sex is over before they even know what they're doing. Even if orgasm does occur, girls in particular don't know what it is or how to enjoy it fully. Premature ejaculation is the norm for teenage males, and their love-making is unlikely to be very subtle, so orgasm for the female is rare in first-time cases, anyway. What should be a beautiful new experience is lost in the urgency of performing, showing off, reaching climax and generally 'getting it on'.

Apart from immaturity, consider the factor of location. Where do first encounters generally take place? In the back seats of cars or on a lumpy couch. They're usually stealthy and hurried due to proximity of parents, neighbours, police or other adult authority figures. Yet sexual behaviour patterns learnt at this time can inhibit and spoil future interaction if not understood and corrected. The first time is always disappointing and always special. Few people forget who their first time was with, even if it was a one-time thing and the partner never seen again. Perhaps it's best that the first time usually happens for people in their teen years as concepts of 'failure' are not as entrenched then. There are so many 'firsts' in a teenager's life that sex is just one of the many being tried, and there can be little doubt in a teenager's mind that there will be many other chances to experiment further.

There are no ultimate experts in the bedroom, even if the bedroom happens to be a car or garage or park bench — most of us are learning about our bodies, sexuality and loving each other all our lives. For teenagers, it's just another crucial lesson of life that has to be tackled head-on. However, if the attempt is a devastating failure, it can put a young person off sex and/or intimacy for a long time as we saw in the case sample earlier in the chapter.

Pornography

All around you these days are blatant sex images and messages. In general, males are more interested than females in pornography, meaning magazines, stories, videos, live sex shows, etc, and teenagers are no exception. No doubt you have fewer opportunities than adults to indulge in these fantasies due to age restrictions, less money to spend or less freedom. Of course you are curious, and whenever you can get hold of a magazine or book, you express a large part of your sexuality using these stimuli. Most of you will grow out of this as you get older, turning to erotic material only occasionally or using them as marital aids, but some will form a lifetime habit.

This is neither good nor bad as long as it's not excessive. Experts continually contend that there is a definite link between pornography and violence in the community. I would caution you against reading and looking at material that interweaves sex and violence because this puts such ideas into your mind and you may be negatively influenced without knowing it. Monitor your own behaviour in this area as I'm sure you want to stay in control. I have no quarrel with erotic films and pictures as long as children and animals aren't involved. You have to decide these matters for yourself but veer towards moderation to be on the safe side.

In summary, sex is one of a broad spectrum of life experiences that you are confronted with at a time when you're being bombarded with mixed messages, hormonal activity and emotional problems. It is undoubtedly one of the most stressful and most important.

For young girls, sex looms as a fantasy and exciting mystery, something to whisper and giggle about with your friends. You don't think about the physical realities, glossing over these in favour of more romantic details. If not properly tutored, you can adopt the belief system that sex is essentially a matter of male pleasure and female endurance. Many girls who write to me speak of the agony of indecision associated with wanting to please their boyfriends yet not feeling ready to have sex.

For young men, sex at puberty is a much more down-to-earth business. You spend years imagining what it's like to be with a girl and the next few years trying to get one! When it finally happens, you're likely to think afterwards, 'that was quick' while the girl is left wondering 'what happened?' The male is driven by ego and biological urges; the female by her need to capture the male with her desirability. Already, we have the beginnings of the eternal battle of the sexes.

Many of these difficulties cannot be avoided as they are intrinsic to the nature of the 'between' period of life, but they can be softened by love and understanding, compassion and education.

5 Emotions

The book to this point has emphasised that teenage stress is, in the main, emotional stress; therefore, this topic needs its own chapter and thorough discussion. All of the factors examined so far — family conflict, difficulties at school, sexual problems, and simply, the nature of being a teenager — form part of the picture. Now we're going to look more closely at your feelings, the types of emotional hassles you're likely to have, and some general ideas about the nature of emotion and how you can learn to manage it in your life.

Emotions are a crucial part of human existence. There's no escaping their effect at any age, no matter how calm and controlled a person is. Of course, between the ages of thirteen and nineteen, feelings are much closer to the surface than at any other time in life. Your hormones are running wild and you live at their mercy, with mood swings, extremes of emotion and erratic behaviour plaguing you daily. I must make a distinction between the earlier and the later stages of teenage. At the younger end, you're likely to be emotional about entering high school, getting on with your friends, starting to like boys/girls, and dealing with the onset of puberty; at the older end, your concerns are more to do with anxieties about the future, leaving school and/or home, dating and social life, money, and entering adulthood.

Let's look at the emotional areas that all teenagers have

to deal with and some strategies for an easier ride on the roller coaster. There are too many negative emotions to discuss each one here, but let's talk about the key ones. I hasten to add that these emotions are only negative if they're mishandled or felt to excess.

Anger

Our society generally frowns on anger in any form. Let's talk about what it is first, and then how it can be a positive force in your life.

Many of you will have anger stored in your heart and in your body from childhood. In chapter 6, we'll be talking about the link between illness and emotion, but it's important to mention here that anger is the deepest childhood emotion because children are so powerless. They haven't the words or the right to speak their anger, and that anger has to go somewhere. If a child tries to express its angry feelings, it immediately incurs the disapproval, and, in turn, anger of its parents, so it learns very early in life to hide this particular emotion. Very often, it is simply stored in the body to manifest later as unexplained aches and pains. Others rebel and go through years of conflict because they're labelled 'difficult' and non-conformist. Even those children who are more assertive by nature lack the information to argue effectively and still live under the shadow of parents or older siblings in deep, silent anger. The tyranny of authority is a frightening thing, especially for a child, and we all know that those in power often abuse this privilege.

There's the old joke about the man getting told off by his boss at work so he goes home and yells at his wife; she in turn spanks her child, and the child kicks the cat. It's not funny when you think about the truth of this story. It probably happens in every family on a regular basis. We tend to take out our frustrations on those nearest to us and that's why most of our deepest conflicts take place in the home.

The things that cause the most anger in childhood are:

- Being unreasonably criticised or blamed
- Excessive physical punishment
- Being left alone at home too much
- Not being listened to
- Feeling rejected or unloved

Many of these will apply to you as teenagers, but add the following for a more complete picture:

- Feeling disempowered by teachers and parents
- Having too many or unreasonable rules to live by
- Wanting to be independent but still needing things from adults
- Frustration at learning or communication difficulties
- Sexual and emotional tension
- Feeling bossed around

We need to differentiate between anger and temper. Temper is a show of anger, and it is usually excessive because it's often a display of anger that has been suppressed over a time. A child who's stamping its foot, screaming or crying, is 'throwing a tantrum', expressing in the only way available the strength of the emotions felt. This might happen several times a day with an extrovert child but a placid child can only let out its feelings in extreme cases. This is the same with teenagers and adults. It depends on your individual personality.

Temper is generally considered a negative way to express anger — so is there a good way to do it? It's difficult to isolate anger from the whole of the human psyche as our emotions are all linked; for example, anger stems from frustration and can lead to violence; good management of anger comes from a healthy self-esteem which leads to assertiveness. All these will be covered in the course of this chapter but, in regard to anger specifically, a good rule of thumb to remember is that human emotion operates like a pressure-cooker. If pressure is not released, you end up with pea soup on the ceiling! If you can't get out the things that are bugging you, as they happen, eventually you'll explode.

So, good anger management lies in honesty of feeling and

clear communication. More stress is caused by poor communication than any other single factor. Even if you're not popular for saying what you think, you'll be a lot less aggressive and rude if you don't wait till things have deteriorated to such an extent that tensions are high and everyone's on edge.

Anger is a positive force when it is used as a tool of assertiveness, not of abuse or revenge. When you can honestly say to your parents something like, 'Mum, when you baby me in front of my friends, I feel really embarrassed and that makes me angry', you have the beginnings of a dialogue. If, instead, you say, 'I want you to stop treating me like a baby in front of my friends because it gives me the s — s, you silly old bag' you have the beginnings of a battle.

Anger management is a challenge for all of us as anger is primal and basic to humans yet socially unacceptable. It's the same with honesty, a characteristic often valued in theory — only — as true honesty can be very hurtful, we condition ourselves to offer and accept a modified version. When we're angry, this inhibition breaks down and we often blurt out what we really think. This can be very destructive to personal relationships. More on this later in the chapter.

Jealousy and envy

What's the difference? Both have their root in anger and resentment, but jealousy is more general while envy is specific. 'I don't like Bill having more money than me' is an example of jealousy; 'I want Bill's money' constitutes envy. These are both petty and energy-wasting emotions. It is said that jealousy is a natural accompaniment to love, but what kind of love? Possessive love seeks to chain the object of love, be it a person, an animal, a house or any other thing. This stems from insecurity in the lover and disregards the feelings of the loved. It may be acceptable for a short period in a new relationship, but if it continues, it can become a destructive force, in some cases, obsessive. Think of movies like *Play Misty For Me* and *Fatal Attraction*. If you saw those films, would you consider that those women really loved the guys or did they want something from them they couldn't give? I'll leave you to arrive at your own answer to that one.

Jealousy doesn't only occur in love or sexual relationships, but can manifest in family life, as we saw earlier with the second child syndrome, where the younger brother was jealous of the older one's achievements. It's also quite common for one child to be possessive over a parent and resent any love shown to or from a sibling. One of the most common examples of family jealousy occurs when a new baby is brought home, especially if the older child was the only one for a few years. If this isn't handled right, it can cause a tremendous amount of hostility between the children as the years pass.

There are as many examples of jealousy as there are types of people in this world. Because teenagers reside in an uncertain, insecure world, you are likely to be prey to this unworthy emotion. It would be foolish of me to suggest that you can simply eradicate it, but keep in mind its negative properties and try to minimise it as much as possible.

Envy is even worse because it adds an acquisitive component. The next time you feel tempted to envy someone or something, remember this: you can't get what someone else has in isolation. Would you be prepared to swap your existence for theirs? For example, how do you know what lies behind the front door of that mansion that you keep driving past and longing for? Those people might be utterly miserable. Would you still want to live there if you knew that? Envy is also illogical. We all get what we deserve, what we've earned in our lives, so, instead of wishing for someone else's property, why not think of a way to get it yourself? A lot of vandalism is caused by envy, stemming from such thoughts as, 'If I can't have a Rolls, I'll damage any that I see parked in the street'; 'Why shouldn't I rip off that house?

Those people can afford it. It's okay to steal from rich people because I'm poor'. You must see that these are weak excuses for taking what other people have earned. And if they got their possessions by unfair means or if they have more than they should, that's their lookout. Life will make them pay in other ways. There are many injustices in this world that are worth fighting for but it's not up to you to redress the balance in this area, and if you do it by being destructive or criminal, you'll only be hurting yourself.

Fear

Here, I'm not speaking of fear in the physical sense but in the psychological. If a stranger chases you up a dark street, only an idiot would suggest that you shouldn't be afraid. But psychological fear stems from insecurity and self-doubt, over which you have control. You shape your feelings with your thoughts. You probably don't believe this at your age, but take my word for it for the time being. I read once that the word FEAR stands for False Evidence Appearing Real. In my writings, I refer to the fantasy of fear. Fear only exists in the mind and is directly linked to negative thinking. When you say that you are 'afraid' to do something, what you're really saying is that you don't believe you can. That belief becomes reality for you and you don't even try after that.

People who succeed are those who recognise the underlying fear but refuse to give in to it. It's like stress itself. You need it to motivate you, to give you the impetus to get moving, but too much of it works against you — as in the case of severe stagefright for performers or physical blocks in athletes.

Another well-known saying about fear is 'The only thing to fear is fear itself'. Without fear, we might be foolhardy; with too much, it cripples us and prevents us from living life fully.

Doubt and negative thinking

These are directly linked to fear. Fear has a certain set of physiological components, such as sweaty hands, physical coldness and racing heartbeat, but doubt and negative thinking are totally mind-games. They are the enemy of joy and happiness and success, because every time you try to do something new or take a chance, your negative ego 'speaks' to you in words such as 'You can't do this', 'Who do you think you are?', 'You're heading for a fall'.

Every day of your life, you'll be assaulted by negative thinking and behaviour from others. When people say to me, 'This psychology stuff is just brainwashing', I say, 'Of course it is! What else have we all had since birth, and most of it negative?' Conditioning goes on from birth to death, and you absorb millions of negative beliefs in one lifetime. You then act out these self-defeating ideas in the form of negative behaviour and think in terms that can be called negative self-talk, such as 'You're so stupid', 'What makes you think you can do this?', 'No-one likes you', 'You're ugly'.

Positive thinking seeks to redress the balance and to reprogramme some of these self-defeating ideas. Negative thinking is linked to poor self-esteem — again! If you love and respect yourself, you don't entertain destructive ideas about yourself and your efforts, appearance, behaviour, and so on. At your age, it's very tempting to be down on yourself on a daily basis, but please fight it so that you can face the challenges of teenage with a straight back, clear eye and the confidence of a winner.

Guilt

Guilt is different from remorse. It doesn't mean that you're sorry if you hurt someone or do the wrong thing. That's remorse. Guilt is a very destructive and irrational emotion.

It usually doesn't link to any reason; for example, some people feel guilty for just being alive! I have to say it yet again: we feel guilty because we feel inferior, 'no good', less than other people. It's often instilled in childhood by overly critical or overstrict parents. If you're put down continuously, told you're useless, lazy, dumb or similar, you'll naturally believe it and grow up with these negative ideas about yourself. Some people accept the responsibility for everything that goes wrong with and around them, which is clearly not rational. I don't know if it's possible to eradicate guilt in your life totally, but be aware of it. Accept the blame if you know you did something wrong, but live by the values of honesty and justice, firstly with yourself and then others.

Anxiety

This is an umbrella term for the phobias, worries and doubts that plague all of us, but especially teenagers. Anxiety is a crippling emotion that can render a person totally dysfunctional. Let's look at some examples.

Phobias are specific fears of such things as insects or flying or lifts or open spaces. Some are very minor and can be easily controlled; others are very serious and prevent sufferers from living normal lives. Two examples are agoraphobics, who cannot leave the house because of the fear of anxiety attacks, and people with obsessive-compulsive disorders, who clean their homes or certain rooms or appliances several times a day because they're convinced that dust can kill or they think their environment cannot ever get clean enough, no matter what they do. Anorexia is an eating disorder but, in its essence, it is also about anxiety, the anxiety of being overweight (see chapter 6).

Most of us suffer anxiety in its milder forms, however, and for teenagers, it is almost a chronic condition. There's anxiety about your looks, being liked, doing well in school, getting a job, family problems, and lots more. As with guilt, I don't think we can ever learn to live totally without anxiety, perhaps because it is so much a part of the human psyche. I always advise that worry is 100 per cent useless and, in fact, creates a second problem — the one you originally had plus the worry you've now added.

Anxiety is not related to real problems, such as a mother worrying about her child's safety; rather, it stems from self-doubt and insecurity. There may be times in life when worry is inevitable, as in the case of having to face an exam in a subject that you're weak in, but how will it help?

Regret is another form of anxiety. It's caused by living in the past and is just as futile as worrying about the future. You only own this moment, and if you live it well, all your other moments will be good, too. There is nothing you can do to undo the past. Regret is an attempt to rationalise an event with the benefit of hindsight, yet you are a different person in the present, as you review the past.

Positive thought is far more effective than worry, and we'll look at this in detail in chapter 8.

Conflict

In a chapter on emotion, we cannot omit this important subject, one already discussed in chapter 2 in the context of family life, and in chapter 3 in the context of school. Here, we're going to look at the handling of it in specific terms. We call this conflict resolution, and it can take many forms.

It stands to reason that you can't deal with conflict if you're emotionally upset, so the first requirement for effective conflict resolution is to calm down. Then, you need to be clear with the other person what the points of conflict actually are — outline these and then take them one at a time, resolving each before moving on. If you think about it, most conflict operates in chaos: tempers fly, voices are raised and nothing at all is settled. At your age, I daresay you settle most of your conflicts that way. Dad says to be home at ten, you argue, he yells at you to do as you're told, you slam out of the house, and your relationship has just received another body blow. Let's take that same scenario in the form of a dialogue and see how it might go differently.

You're about to go out. Dad says, 'I want you home at ten tonight.'

You: 'But I'm going to a movie in town. It won't be finished till eleven, then I've got to get a bus home.'

Dad: 'Well, you know the rules. Ten o'clock on a weeknight. You shouldn't even be going out at all. What about your homework?'

You: 'Dad, I told you. This is a film for English, a school excursion.'

Dad: 'Why didn't you say that in the first place? What time does the movie come out? I'll pick you up.'

You: 'Dad, I feel stupid having my dad pick me up. I'll get the bus with all the others. I promise we won't go for coffee or anything, okay?'

Dad: 'All right. Have a good time.'

This scene could come out in a thousand different ways, but what are the key issues?
- Poor communication
- Homework and going out on weeknights
- Curfew rules
- Teenager wanting to be independent yet trusted

Conflict is part of the human condition but remember, when you shout, argue and get abusive, you've lost your right to be heard reasonably.

Some of you are no doubt thinking that you've tried a quiet approach but have been ignored or shouted down yourselves. You know your own parent(s) and can devise a system of conflict resolution that works for you.

Love

This is such a misused term that it has almost become meaningless. I can tell you what I think love is but it may not mean anything like that to you. To me, love is putting another first, not in a self-sacrificing or self-destructive way but, whether it's a friend, a parent or a special person in your life, love empowers you to care for their welfare, even if it's difficult for you. For example, in my opinion, if a person you love needs you, you go — but there is one proviso: it has to be reciprocal, because if the loved one doesn't care about you in return, you're just being used. I heard a great definition recently, 'Love is being kind to each other'.

When you're young, you can't always make this distinction but that's also part of the growing up process. You trust the wrong people, you get hurt, let down, disillusioned, swear you'll never love again, and then start the whole cycle once more the next time you meet someone you like. Relationships are challenging at any age so don't despair — you get to do this for the rest of your life! Joy and hurt, struggle and success, pain and happiness all work hand in hand. The Bible says that 'in the midst of life, we are in death'. That sums up the contradictory nature of life. Everything seems to work in extremes. How many times have you despaired of a situation and were just about to give up when the whole thing turned around? Or perhaps you have worked terribly hard towards a goal only to keep failing, then suddenly something different and better appears on the horizon.

Relationships are the most strenuous challenges in our lives because of the erratic quality of human nature, because so much emotion is usually involved, and because, as we've seen, emotions are irrational. All the things that cause problems in family life (see chapter 2) stem from these factors. With sisters and brothers, we experience jealousy, competitiveness, anger; with parents, frustration, defiance, resentment; with friends, hurt, envy, rivalry.

We also spoke, however, of the power of love. As with all abstracts, love cannot be measured or analysed, but we can see its effects in action. We see the devotion of mothers, nurses, nuns, missionaries, those who care for children, the aged and the sick. Every single day, we see incredible feats of selfless love as demonstrated by ordinary men and women.

If, as a human race, we ever fail to notice or believe this, then we are truly lost in this world.

In chapter 4, we discussed sex specifically and I said that the nicest sex occurs between people who care about each other. This might sound very old-fashioned, but I don't say it from a moral or religious standpoint. Even in terms of sensual pleasure, sex is much better when love is also a participant. Sure, there is such a thing as animal lust and it has its place even in the most decorous relationships, but such feelings as tenderness, generosity and caring are only possible with the presence of love. That's why it's so important not to give yourself away too freely. Value yourself.

Friendship is one of our most precious gifts but, as with love, there are many definitions for it. Being mates, social acquaintances, colleagues — these are all forms of friendship, but in its purest and deepest form, it is akin to love, with the same elements of caring, sharing and giving of oneself. Both love and friendship can be selfish, conditional and competitive, but they can also be forgiving and generous and compassionate. They are gifts that cannot be demanded or forced. If you are lucky enough to find them as you go along, you then have to be worthy enough to hang on to them. My policy now is that if something or someone leaves my life, I let it go freely as the timing could be off or I may have damaged it without even meaning to, and trying to hang on will only hurt me and others more. Of course, I could not have done this at your age or even up till a few years ago. It's all trial and error, so learn to forgive yourself as soon as possible. Every night before you sleep, let go of all the hurts and disappointments of the day, forgive others and yourself, then sleep peacefully, confident that tomorrow will be a bright new day which you can begin with a clean slate.

Death and loss

One of the most emotional experiences in life is the loss or death of a loved one. If any of you have lost a parent, you will know that it is devastating and unforgettable. Life goes on, as they say, but there is always an emptiness that nothing and no-one can ever fill. I was already twenty-three when my mother died but, as I had not known my father, she was everything to me. My half-brother and sister were only seven and nine and their lives were changed irrevocably. There are whole books written about children who lose one or more parent, either through death or other forms of loss. The casualties include innocence and trust. How can a child ever trust love when it is snatched away in the shape of a beloved parent? Surely parents are fortresses against loneliness and hurt, yet suddenly that security is gone.

My brother and sister have both suffered emotional problems. I tried to be their surrogate mother, but no love I could give was able to make up for what they'd lost. My brother alienates people before relationships can begin so he doesn't ever have to lose anyone. My sister is much more accessible and therefore well-liked, but she dabbles emotionally, never committing fully so that she is always in control. Two different approaches but the same pain.

Whenever death comes, it is painful, and obviously, the closer the person was to you, the deeper the hurt. For a child, it may be a beloved pet dying or a babysitter leaving or moving away from a familiar area. Apart from the death of my mother, the great losses for me were my pet dogs. Five years ago, my golden retriever died suddenly and unexpectedly and then, three years ago, my old labrador died at the grand age of fifteen. The emotions were different in each case but I can never forget the shock and the pain. I cradled Cassie, the retriever, on my lap as we were driven to the pet cemetery, a two-hour trip while my sweet dog stiffened and went cold in my arms. Henry, the old lab, at least died peacefully in his sleep, at the end of an interesting and full life.

Until my mother died, Death was just a word to me, as it no doubt is to those of you who have not experienced it first-hand. When it strikes, it feels as if you're dead yourself, and for a very long time afterwards, you feel numb and unable to believe that the person you love has really gone. The more information you have, the better you can cope, although nothing can insulate you from the pain. I didn't know much about the bereavement process when I lost my mum at twenty-three but I was better equipped to work through my dogs' deaths because of my training and study.

There has been a lot of research into death and bereavement. We know now that there are definite stages of response after a death takes place. There's the initial shock I've mentioned, then there's a stage of denial during which there's an emotional block set up to avoid the terrible pain. This block can take many forms, but in my experience of working with the bereaved, I find it's often done through keeping busy. At first, it's making the funeral arrangements and participating in the practical rituals of burial, then it's going back to work or school and so on, the plan being to outrun pain. It works for a while, sometimes years, but eventually a trigger brings the bereaved person face to face with the memory of the loss, and the dam bursts. This is healthy and necessary because only when the pain is embraced and released, can a new beginning truly occur. Knowing these stages, you can hasten the process by facing your loss head-on. Now, I give myself a 'mourning day' if I suffer any sort of loss. During that day, I weep and remember and fully immerse myself in the grief but, by the next day, I can begin anew, not forgetting but moving on, as life dictates we must.

In the next chapter, we will explore the subjects of suicide and life after death.

Violence and crime

We saw earlier that anger stems from frustration. From anger comes violence. What is frustration basically? It's a feeling of helplessness, powerlessness and victimisation. We have seen the effects of these in previous chapters. But how does it actually work in a real situation? Frustration builds up like an unseen pressure; anger is the natural follow-on. Release doesn't always come immediately; for example, you can still be carrying the anger caused by an event that happened years ago. I'm not talking about grudges or even resentment, which is a lot easier to identify. I mean deep-seated anger such as that felt over the death of a parent or being neglected or abused, feeling unloved or physically abandoned, over poverty and cruelty. It doesn't only come from big things; even a number of small hurts can build up like a house of cards or a Lego construction.

Good anger management allows for the communication and release of hurts and irritations but, as we've seen, most of us are not taught how to handle our angry feelings. If there is sufficient anger in a person, it explodes in the form of violence. Let me tell you a fascinating true story.

A French family was travelling some distance from their home to go on holiday. There was Mum, Dad and two little boys. The boys began the journey in the back of the car but, as is usual with small children, the two began fighting and finally Mum insisted that the toddler move to the front. The other boy, about four years old, was left in the back for the entire trip, lasting several hours. If he tried to speak he was shushed, and he remained staring at the backs of his three family members, feeling totally alienated. When they arrived at their destination, the mother turned around and told the boy he had been very good throughout the trip. This was the trigger that set off the explosion. The boy reached into a bag of provisions, grabbed a bottle of milk and slashed his mother with the broken glass, killing her.

Frustration — anger — violence. You might argue that the boy was emotionally disturbed beforehand, and that would be a valid point. He was undoubtedly suffering from sibling jealousy at the arrival of the new child and this was the last event in a long chain of frustration. A good illustration of the negative power of stored-up anger.

Of course, if we take this to the extreme, we can look at psychopaths, serial killers, rapists and other violent criminals. No-one who terrifies, tortures or kills other living creatures can possibly be 'normal'. We all have our idiosyncrasies and neuroses but we find reasonable ways to deal with our angers and disappointments. Why do some people turn to crime? It must either be in their make-up, as in mental disease, or it's accumulated negative energy. We need to be less afraid of our true feelings as it is the suppression of them that leads to destructive behaviours. It's okay to be honest in your anger. I did suggest earlier that truthful, if unpleasant, remarks can often be expressed in an angry situation, and that's a good opportunity for 'clearing the air', as long as it isn't done nastily or cruelly. In order to avoid this, annoying incidents should be addressed as they occur and not allowed to bank up.

Emotion is just one of the many ways that human beings can communicate with each other. We all feel the need to reach out and we shouldn't be afraid of our feelings. Sometimes, they seem too powerful to handle and we either hide them, pretend we don't care, or we lash out at others and the whole world. Some of you are bound to be more emotional than others, just as some of you have dark hair and some are fair. One is not better than the other — each is different. Only when emotion is totally out of control and excessive is it negative. You don't want it to rule your life, and even during the teenage years, it is possible to keep from emotional chaos. And yet, spontaneity is a wonderful quality, one that can be fully enjoyed at your age. As with so many things, balance is the key. Spontaneity is good but impulsiveness is not; being expressive is great but being an emotional victim is not, and so on.

You will find these answers for yourself as you go along. Follow the suggestions in this book step by step and you should start to make choices for yourself. Especially if you're at the older end of the teenage years, you will feel less and less like a victim and more and more like a mature individual person, who enjoys life and isn't afraid of it. If you're at the younger end, you have to be content with other people's decisions for the present but you have the power to make the journey tougher or smoother for all concerned.

A sense of humour goes a long way, and laughter is one of the most therapeutic things available to us. When you're feeling crowded, a walk by the ocean is most healing, or just go and sit in a quiet park for a few minutes. Music is terrific for the troubled soul, but perhaps you could try some of the softer kind occasionally! There is beauty and help all around you. Just reach out for it.

6 Health

Health is an important consideration at any age, but the habits you set now are going to affect you for many years to come. So in this chapter, I'll look at the key issues in this area, starting with the effect of emotions on health.

Emotions and health

Research has established that about 85 per cent of all illness is 'psychosomatic', but this doesn't mean that the illness is imagined or isn't genuine. It actually means that a large percentage of human sickness stems from an emotional base. We have already discussed the way that anger can be stored in the body and bring on physical symptoms such as headache, stomach upset and even serious disease. In chapter 1, in the general description of stress and its effects, I explained that stress breaks down the immune system in the body and leaves it vulnerable to infection, viruses and health breakdown. Often, when we catch a cold or develop 'flu, it's after a period of feeling rundown or overdoing things, in other words, living with undue stress.

There are many books written on this subject, and they seek to explain every ailment in emotional terms. For example, constipation is related to an inability to 'let go'; stiff and sore knees reflect an inflexible attitude; skin rash denotes impatience and restlessness. Not all of this is medically provable, but I do think it's logical and reasonable to believe that our emotional selves cannot be separated from our physical beings. One particular area that seems to be undisputed is to do with the link between stress and serious diseases like cancer, AIDS and heart trouble. Prevention is the answer, and education about health matters, and living in harmony.

Stress and health

Stress has a strong effect on the emotions, as we saw extensively in the last chapter. It's a circular influence. Too much stress results in depression, anxiety and other negative emotions; emotional excesses cause stress, and so it goes. You need to understand this relationship and the role it plays in your life.

The best way to gauge your general well-being is to study the amount of tension in your body. You can feel this simply by awareness. If you're old enough to drive, try deliberately relaxing your body as you drive along. You'll be amazed at how much tension was present before you 'let go'. Feel it in the grip of your hands on the steering-wheel, the way your back sits against the seat and the tightness in your neck. Most of us walk around with that level of tension until we do something about it.

The best 'cure' is not to let the tension build up in the first place. But, if you are already tense or stressed, and you're worried that it's affecting your health, try meditation, deep breathing exercises, yoga, regular therapeutic massage, relaxation procedures, counselling, whatever you need.

Relaxation exercises

1. I surrender myself. *(Slight pause)*
   My right arm is heavy — my right hand is heavy — my right arm and hand are heavy — my right arm and hand

are sinking into the ground. *(Pause)* My left arm is heavy — my left hand is heavy — my left arm and hand are heavy — my left arm and hand are sinking into the ground. *(Pause)* My right leg is heavy — my right foot is heavy — my right leg and foot are heavy — my right leg and foot are sinking into the ground. *(Pause)* My left leg is heavy — my left foot is heavy — my left leg and foot are heavy — my left leg and foot are sinking into the ground. *(Pause)* My arms are heavy — my legs are heavy — my arms and legs are heavy — my body is heavy. *(Pause)* I surrender myself — my body is heavy. *(10 second pause)*

II. I surrender myself — my body is heavy. *(Pause)*

My right arm is warm — my right hand is warm — my right arm is nice and warm — my right arm and hand are warm. *(Pause)*

My left arm is warm — my left hand is warm — my left arm is nice and warm — my left arm and hand are warm. *(Pause)*

My left leg is warm — my left foot is warm — my left foot is nice and warm — my left leg and foot are warm. *(Pause)*

My arms are warm — my legs are warm — my centre is warm — my centre is nice and warm. *(Pause)*

I surrender myself — my centre is warm. *(10 second pause)*

III. I surrender myself — my body is warm — my centre is warm. *(Pause)*

My pulse is calm — my pulse is steady and calm — my pulse is steady — my pulse is calm. *(Pause)*

I surrender myself — my pulse is calm. *(10 second pause)*

IV. I surrender myself — my body is heavy — my centre is warm — my pulse is calm. *(Pause)*

The air is breathing me — the air is breathing me — the air is breathing me — the air is breathing me. *(Pause)*

I surrender myself — the air is breathing me. *(Now 30 second pause)*

V. My face is cool — my face is nice and cool — my face is cool. *(Pause)* Make fists. *(Actually make a fist slowly and tightly, and release slowly)* Make fists. *(Actually make a fist slowly and tightly, and release slowly)* Take a deep breath, stretch arms, legs and body, yawn, stretch fingers and toes, wriggle body. *(Again a 30 second pause)*
Open eyes slowly.

This whole relaxation exercise takes up about 10 minutes. Be kind to yourself, give yourself a 10-minute present once in a while!

Unfortunately, in our society, many teenagers turn to negative, short-term solutions for dealing with stress such as smoking, alcohol and drugs. Let's firstly look at the nature of addiction and then take each of these major examples in turn.

Addiction

If I had to describe the meaning of addiction in one word, it would be dependence — dependence on something or someone outside yourself. Addiction isn't only needing things that are 'bad'. You can also be addicted to positive and good things. Anything done to excess can become a need, and if you can't give it up or do without it, it's got you hooked. When we hear about addictions, it's usually about smoking, drinking and drugs, but if you were to pray all day every day or think about nothing but sex or eat ten meals daily, these behaviours could all be considered obsessive and, therefore, addictive.

If you have what is called an 'addictive personality' you will tend to give away your power to some external thing that you then develop a constant craving for. Another teenager could try the same thing and take it or leave it in the future. That's why experimenting with drugs or alcohol can be risky, although, as I've said before, natural at your age. You see why I harp on this point of knowing yourself, because there's no value in comparing yourself to the norm or to other teenagers. You are unique and need to guard your health zealously as you need your body for a lifetime. Although your true self resides within, you can't do much in life without a healthy body and mind. So let's look now at specific common addictions and what you can do if you want to kick the habit.

Smoking

I doubt if there's a teenager, past or present, who hasn't tried smoking at some stage. Many of you would have experimented even earlier. My one abortive attempt happened when I was about eight. I don't even remember where I got the cigarettes, but I locked myself in my room and lit up. Needless to say I hated it, coughed and spluttered smoke everywhere, and put the cigarette out straight away. That would have been the end of it except that a small piece of hot ash fell onto my pillow and burnt the cover. The next day, my mother caught sight of this and I got a long lecture about the dangers of smoking. Many years later, in my late teens, I took up smoking again for a short period. Luckily, I discovered that I'm not the addictive type and I never developed a chemical dependence. I was only ever a social smoker, going through a packet maybe every week or two. Eventually, there was no longer any point buying cigarettes and I haven't touched one now for years.

Looking back, I have to ask myself why then did I smoke at all? If I wasn't hooked on nicotine, which is, by the way, as addictive as heroin, why did I bother to buy cigarettes and go through the motions? To feel I belonged in a social group when everyone else was smoking? To overcome feelings of stress in awkward situations? To give my hands something to do when I felt shy or uncomfortable? I don't know. If any of you are in the same situation, think about your reasons and perhaps you'll stop wasting your money and time on an activity you don't even really enjoy.

If, however, you're chemically dependent, it's a more difficult story. I was asked to devise a Quit programme for a weekend seminar a few years ago. Here it is. It might be helpful to you as one possible approach.

Quit programme

The following exercise aims to encourage the smoker to examine his/her reasons for smoking, how and why he/she began, and his/her emotional contact with cigarettes. It is not intended as a deep therapy programme but rather as an examination of motives and goals in the pursuance of what is one of our most common social habits. If possible do this with a friend or relative who is a fellow-smoker.

The origins of the habit
- At what age did I begin smoking?
- Was it my own idea, or who got me started?
- How did I feel when I first began to smoke?
- What age was I when I began to smoke?
- Did my parents smoke?
- Did the friends in my group smoke?

Motivation for the habit
- What do I like about smoking?
- What do I dislike about smoking?
- What do I dislike most of all about the feedback I get from my non-smoking friends?
- How many do I smoke in any one given day?
- Where and when do I do most of my smoking?
- Is there a link in my life between stress and smoking?
- Is there a link in my life between eating and smoking?
- Is there a link in my life between alcohol and smoking?
- Do the people I see most smoke?
- Does my spouse smoke?

- How do I feel about my children smoking?
- Do I smoke at my place of work?
- Do I resent the amount of money I spend on cigarettes?
- Do I worry about my health because of smoking?
- Do I suffer any physical symptoms because of smoking?
- Have I ever had an embarrassing moment related to smoking?

Goals for Kicking the habit
- Why would I like most to give up smoking?
- Of all the people I know, who tells me the most often that I should give up smoking?
- Am I influenced to give up smoking by the media?
- What do I fear most about having to give up smoking?
- How do I think I am going to feel for the first few days of withdrawal?
- How do I think I am going to feel if I successfully complete the withdrawal process?
- Am I worried that I am going to gain weight if I give up smoking?
- Have I got anything in mind that I can do instead of smoking? E.g. at a party, pub or at work.

Self image versus social image
- Do I like myself? Do I think I am a good person?
- How do I think I feel in a crowd?
- How do I feel at a party if I do not know anybody?
- Does smoking give me confidence?
- Am I worried that I am going to look stupid without a cigarette in my hand?
- Is smoking a way to pose, to look cool?
- Do cigarettes help me to make conversation, e.g. offering a cigarette or offering to light a cigarette?
- Am I a nervous and restless person?
- Am I a tense person?
- Do I worry too much?
- Do I get bored easily?
- Do I actually feel better after smoking?

Coping with withdrawal (exchange ideas and discuss with others)
- Practical tips and ideas for quitting
- How to alleviate stress during the crucial first days:
  relaxation
  meditation
  massage
- How to develop 'distractions', particularly keeping the hands busy
- Occupy the time when you would normally be smoking, e.g. at the pub, play darts while you are having a beer
- Develop an attitude of self-love so that smoking becomes undesirable because it does not nurture the body but rather harms it
- Most importantly, work at fitness of the body, as exercise relieves tension and also a healthy body craves less the dependencies of such things as tobacco, alcohol, drugs and excess food

There are simpler methods you can adopt to give up smoking. The Government Health Department has a kit that you can have free of charge, which contains brochures and equipment to help you. There are courses you can attend, substitutes to smoke which will gradually wean you off the habit, and even special sweets to suck every time you feel like a cigarette. So, if you're serious about quitting, there's certainly no excuse. You're at the perfect age to stop before your addiction is fully entrenched.

Why quit? You're no doubt sick of hearing how bad smoking is for your health. Youth often feels itself invincible and talk of disease and death falls on deaf ears. I'm not in favour of scare tactics as a form of education although advertising campaigns that use them, such as the famous AIDS one showing the Grim Reaper bowling, are huge successes. I prefer to talk to you as intelligent, rational people who will listen to reason if it's put to you with respect and caring. So, rather than lecture to you about the hazards of smoking, and give you a whole lot of information that you've heard a thousand times before, I'd rather suggest you think about why you want to smoke instead of focusing on why you should stop. The teenage psyche does not respond well to being told it 'ought' or it 'should'. It just makes you want to do that very thing all the more. But, if you yourself decide on a course of action, it's much more likely to last. If you're thirteen to fifteen and smoking, you're probably not going to listen to anything I might say about smoking. It makes you feel good, helps you to fit in and is the 'done' thing. But if you are sixteen to nineteen, you can make these decisions for yourself, based on self-love and not self-destruction or peer pressure.

My final words on smoking then are — consider the health aspects; only do it if you know why and make a conscious decision to continue; reach out for help if you decide you want to stop; remember, you can stop more easily now while you're in the early stages of the addiction and you may not be able to later in life.

Alcohol

This is a broader subject. Again, as with smoking, most of you try it at some time. The 'why' of it is also likely to be similar: wanting to hide from the reality of life's difficulties, wanting to belong and not be considered a wowser, wanting to do something you think is 'grown-up'. Beyond these similarities, the issues surrounding the drinking of alcohol take on several other complexities. I'm not saying one is better or worse than the other, and, sadly, they usually go hand in hand. Let's look at the factors surrounding alcohol use in general and some specific problems that are associated with its abuse.

Firstly, we live in a society that actively encourages not only the drinking of alcohol but excessive intake. What is the chief topic of conversation in most homes and offices on a Monday morning? What everyone did on the weekend and how 'blotto' they got? Now, here's a reasonable question to which I would love an answer: Why is getting drunk something to boast about? No, I'm not being sarcastic — I'm deadly serious. What achievement is it? How does it take any brains or courage or resourcefulness? I have never been able to figure out why people always look so pleased with themselves when they talk about getting drunk. Have you ever done this? You only have to see yourself in an inebriated state to know how illogical it is to boast about it; you only have to live through one real hangover to ask why on earth you'd want to put yourself through that on a regular basis; you only have to be around a person out of control through liquor to swear off the stuff for life. The 'respect yourself' ad campaign on TV shows this very clearly.

Don't get me wrong. I got drunk lots of times when I was your age, and I don't regret it because it's all part of growing-up and experimenting, as I've said repeatedly through this book. But a key difference is that I didn't do it as a way of life. It really scares me when teeenagers go out on the weekend specifically to get drunk. It scares me because I wonder why you can't think of more interesting things to do. I wonder whose example you're following, and I hope you aren't setting up a habit for life.

Why do people drink in the first place? Social acceptance; peer pressure; boredom; chemical dependence; emotional stress; to lose inhibitions; to alleviate depression and anxiety. At your age, any one of these reasons is enough to get you started. Why some teenagers drink and others don't is a complex question. Another is, why is it that some of you can take one drink and leave it at that while others need to get blind drunk? As with smoking, alcohol can be very addictive, both physically and emotionally. It's a quick fix for all of life's problems, but think of this: when you sober up, you are still you, and you still have the same problems that you tried to drown. Wouldn't it be better to find a more positive, long-term solution?

At the risk of repetition, the key is balance. Have a drink, by all means, if you're of age, or if you're drinking at home with your parents' permission. The powerful need in you to rebel and break the rules makes you want to drink illegally as much as the desire for grog. In fact, many teenagers tell me they don't even like the taste of alcohol, and when I ask the obvious question, 'Then why drink?' I get this answer: 'Aw, everyone does it. It makes you feel good.' Yes, alcohol does give you a feeling of euphoria, but that's only true up to a certain point, and then you start to go downhill. If you ignore the warning signs and keep drinking, you finish up loud, aggressive, belligerent, bilious, maudlin, sick, and, finally, unconscious.

It's not alcohol itself that's 'bad', it's the abuse of it. The signs to watch out for in your drinking habits are: feeling that you 'need' to drink regularly and/or excessively; being a 'cupboard drinker', sneaking alcohol when it isn't readily available; drinking alone; drinking when you're depressed or scared. If you're doing any of these, you may have an alcohol dependency problem, whatever your age. As with your adult counterparts, being prepared to recognise and admit this is the first step to recovery.

But even if you believe your drinking is manageable, try to keep to the guidelines for safe amounts. Alcohol can be damaging to your health even in small doses, depending on factors such as how often you drink, your body weight and size, and your general health. One major difference between smoking and drinking is that with the former, you only hurt yourself; if you drink to excess, you can do damage in a number of ways, such as driving a car when under the influence and causing a fatal accident. If you have lived with alcohol problems in your family, you know the terrible toll excessive drinking takes on everyone in the home, not just the drinker. We saw in chapter 2 that parents are our role-models and we tend to mimic their habits, ideas and behaviours. This applies to destructive actions as much as healthy and positive ones.

Alcohol can bring on behavioural problems and can itself become one. It's often said that under the influence of alcohol, drinkers feel braver, more confident, more truthful. If you need alcohol to achieve these feelings on an ongoing basis, you are probably relying on it and that can become a problem, if not now then in later years. It might take you a while to wake up to it but, when you do, I hope that you will either give up drinking altogether, cut down or get help from a professional source. If you find a way to manage alcohol in your life now, it can be a pleasant, social friend to you in the coming years, not a tyrannical master.

Drugs

Nicotine and alcohol are as addictive as any of the drugs I'm going to mention in this section, but because these two are so much a part of Australian society, we often forget that fact. The majority of you will not have tried anything stronger than marijuana, and even then, on a minor, experimental basis, but some of you reading this book may be addicted to hard drugs, may be dealers, pushers or junkies. I can't supply all the answers for you but there are many agencies and organisations that are equipped to advise you on how to kick your habits or how to live with them more safely. I can only urge you to reach out for help, because you care enough about yourself not to want to damage your health, wreck your relationships and sabotage your future. Don't take the cop-out road of blaming life or your parents or the 'system' for your problems. Own them and fix them.

For the rest of you, I can only say that if you know the facts and you still choose to experiment or allow yourself to become addicted, I hope you stop before it's too late, as once you're in the clutches of an addiction, it's very hard to escape its grasp.

To most of you, words like heroin, crack, cocaine, ecstasy

and LSD belong in American TV jargon. They're not part of your reality, and I'm pleased to be able to say that. In years to come, this may no longer be so, but it's going to depend on our current drug control strategies. When I was at school, hard drugs were unheard of in schools or social venues; now, they are much more readily available. Taking drugs isn't like smoking or drinking where you can take a drink or a puff of a cigarette and then reject it as a habit. If you are turning to 'getting high' as a way to escape daily problems, your short-term solution may become a long-term nightmare.

In Australia, hard drugs are not the biggest problem among teenagers — it's marijuana smoking and glue/petrol sniffing that goes on in our schools and at teenage parties, behind the garage and anywhere else that's away from adult supervision. Joints are commonly passed around at parties, and, again, most of you will not resist the temptation to try them. Unlike alcohol, pot is a passive drug, decidedly anti-social, which begs the question: why would young people want to get together and sit around in a daze rather than talking, dancing, laughing? Are your stresses so severe that you can only have a good time when you're 'out of it'? I've always preferred to get high on life, but perhaps that's a naive suggestion for me to make to you. You have to like yourself, living and life in order to get up in the morning just happy to be alive and unafraid of challenges and setbacks. Okay, I accept that it's probably far more important at your age to be liked by your friends and try everything that's offering, even if it's harmful to you. Perhaps this following story will influence you more than anything I could say.

After a major operation I had a few years ago, I had to undergo a programme of physical exercises which included hydrotherapy. One day, in the pool, I saw a young man being helped into the water by two nurses. He was blind and, I assumed, a victim of a car accident. Later, I asked one of the nurses about him and found out that he had been into sniffing a well-known spray cooking product. He and his friends got high on the stuff and, because of prolonged abuse, the boy was now blind and severely brain-damaged. I was astounded that what he thought was a harmless piece of fun could totally wreck his life in that way. Do you think for one minute that he would have done it if he had known the consequences? That's why we have to talk about these matters openly, and not shy from them. You might very well sniff glue or petrol or whatever else someone tells you will give you a high simply because you're bored and looking for a different kick to try, but next time you feel inclined, remember the boy in the pool. I shall certainly never forget the look of lost despair on his face.

If we as adults can help you through the maze of your teenage years, offer joy in place of despair, enjoyable activities instead of mindless games and violent movies, love you rather than condemn, we might be able to steer you towards some less self-destructive experimental activities. We don't want you to contract AIDS, get hooked on drugs, commit suicide, have to get married or be permanently unemployed. Yet, we can only do a part of it — you have to try as well. Remember 'drugs' is a very wide term, covering everything from street drugs to medicine in the chemist shop. It's safer to steer away from even something as mild as aspirin unless you really need it, and never use drugs to heal emotional problems. That can lead you into deep, deep waters, as many people hooked on Serepax and Valium have found after it's too late.

Addiction is a dual-edged sword. Not only do you have to fight the chemical and physical dependence that drugs build up in your body, you also have to break down the emotional need, which is far stronger, and, therefore, a more formidable opponent. I made the point earlier that addiction can relate to almost anything in life, not just the obvious 'bad' things. One common but not so obvious area of addiction is eating. This problem is not confined to teenagers, but eating disorders are almost totally the province of teenage girls and, if not corrected, can continue into mature years.

Eating disorders

The two main ones are anorexia nervosa and bulimia. From my research, I find that they have their root in the same cause: low self-esteem and a desire for self-destruction. Theories are always coming forward citing everything from a chemical imbalance in the body to food allergies, but I trust my own patients, and the data they give me is consistent. In every case, the girl was either overweight or thought she was, with a very low self-image, and was overly-focused on food. Most of you will love to eat and that's how it should be. Your bodies are growing and you need lots of fuel. Also, the more variety you have in your diet, the better (see section on diet).

Eating disorders are really not to do with food but a mismanagement of food. There's no pleasure in eating; rather, food comes to be regarded as the enemy. The anorexic thinks she is very fat, regardless of actual body weight. There was a girl in my class when I was in high school who was always talking about her latest diet. The rest of us used to laugh as she was painfully thin. Of course, we had never heard the word anorexic, but it's clear to me now that my classmate was one. She was very plain and didn't relate well to people, although, on the surface, was cheerful. My other personal experience of anorexia came when I was in hospital once. In my ward was a sufferer. Again, she was excruciatingly thin. At dinner, we sat next to each other at the table and put before us was an extremely plain meat and salad meal. I didn't look round but could feel her shivering with revulsion, trembling at the thought of eating that food. Finally, she ran away from the table without eating one bite. Later, we talked and she explained her condition to me, how she usually hid in the toilet rather than face dinner, how she virtually stopped eating and nearly died, how she had to be admitted to hospital periodically in order to stop herself starving to death. I didn't then have the questions but I often think back and wish I could ask her what caused her self-loathing, for only that could cause a person to endure so much self-inflicted pain.

This was a very severe case but some of you reading this may be experiencing milder forms of the same condition. The symptoms to watch for are: too much concentration on your weight, constantly checking your measurements and always feeling dissatisfied, no matter how thin you are; turning off food more and more, even when you're hungry; associating your weight with your popularity, approval levels, acceptance, desirability, etc.; feeling as if you want to punish yourself by food denial every time something goes wrong in your life.

Bulimia takes a slightly different form. An anorexic is rarely overweight whereas a bulimic can be. This second type of eating disorder is characterised by binges followed by purging, that is, self-induced vomiting. I've been told by sufferers that attacks usually follow a stress event, for example, a disappointment or quarrel. Almost in a trance, a bulimic will eat through a mountain of unrelated food, whatever's in the kitchen or cupboard. It's only after the binge that the bulimic realises what's happened. It then becomes necessary to lose all that's been eaten. Bulimics are often also addicted to diet pills and/or laxatives and diuretics. One patient told me that she'd been told all her life how plain she was, and as she grew up, she believed it totally. Whenever she looked in a mirror, she saw a lumpy, unattractive person. By overeating, she maintained this image in a self-fulfilling prophecy. She believed it so she lived it.

There are, of course, teenagers who simply overeat, and develop weight problems. To understand this, you need to know why you do it. Food is a lot more than just fuel for the body; it's tied up with a lot of emotion and social ritual. It's one of the first comforts we're given as babies and thereafter, in our lives, we tend to turn to food when life gets difficult. It's all right to cheer yourself up with a chocolate bar occasionally, but if it becomes another crutch, you can easily become addicted to food, and all the things I said about addiction will apply here as well.

Diet

You've all heard that a balanced diet is the best for sustained good health. Putting aside eating disorders or overeating, most of you should be able to maintain a daily diet that takes from each of the five main food groups, without giving up any of the things you love. Back to that word again — balance. There's nothing wrong with a hamburger once or even twice a week, but any more than that and your diet is out of whack. This doesn't only apply to so-called fast foods or 'junk' foods; it would be the same if you wanted to eat nothing but fruit or green vegetables all day. You need variety, and to eat food in proportion. You know that if you eat too many chocolate bars you 'break out'. Well, it's the same with other foods, even if the effects are not as visible. To do the many important jobs your body has to each and every day, the right type of fuel is vital. People who wouldn't dream of putting inferior petrol or oil into their motor vehicles don't hesitate to throw down into their stomachs anything they fancy, be it greasy, undercooked, too starchy, or simply too much at one time. Respect your body and it will give you good service till the day you die, and remember that the eating habits you develop now are liable to stay with you throughout your life.

When I was growing up, I was made to eat everything put before me, including vegetables. The rule was: no clean plate, no dessert, and because I was a great fan of vanilla ice-cream, I was willing to suffer through all the other courses. As a result, I now enjoy almost every type of food, and am a very easy dinner guest to cater for. I'm sure at the time I thought my mother was being very hard, but I guess this is a good example of Mother Knows Best. Of course, there's a lot more education about food these days, and there's a much wider selection of menus and dishes in restaurants and private homes, due to the diversification of Australian cuisine through cosmopolitan influences. So, your generation has no doubt developed a more sophisticated palate. Aim for variety, quality and pleasure, and you can't go wrong.

Exercise and sport

Some of you probably hate organised sport, as I did when I was at school. Those of you who don't are lucky because football, hockey, basketball, netball, cricket, etc. provide excellent opportunities for positive exercise: they give you a good workout physically, there's the need for mental concentration, they are fun if you're good at them, you learn important social skills, they're very rewarding to do well, and you always have a worthwhile goal to aim for.

If you don't enjoy school sport, it's because you're not very good at it or you don't like sport in general or you have an unsympathetic teacher. I remember one particular gym mistress I had in high school who was very fit, had been to the Olympics and assumed that everyone had her abilities. Her classes were always first thing on a Friday morning, a time of the week I came to dread. She put us through horrendous workouts, insisted that we try every sport whether we had any aptitude for it or not, and if we said we couldn't do gymnastics she simply came over and pushed us into the desired positions. I'm sure she didn't mean to be cruel but it's an approach that many of you have probably also had to live through — the 'anyone who says they can't do it is a wimp' syndrome. School sport, as with all forms of learning, should be a source of pleasure and fun, of discovery and challenge, not humiliating and painful.

I hope many of you are lucky enough to be attending schools where the environment allows you to learn and develop at your own pace. If not, hold onto the thought that it is possible to undo the harm when you're older. Because of my unfortunate experiences with school sport, I had it fixed in my mind that I was uncoordinated when in fact, as I found a few years ago when I started attending a gym and took aerobics, I have terrific coordination and can really enjoy working my body physically.

However, there is nothing to be ashamed of if you are just not into physical activities. Perhaps you're the bookworm type or prefer playing a musical instrument to playing with a ball; well, that's fine. We're all different and that's what makes us all special. For health purposes, you do need to keep your body moving but you don't need team sport in order to do that. Solitary exercise is my favourite, swimming and walking, as these not only work the body but are soothing and relaxing to the mind. As long as you're not a couch potato, and you keep active in a day-to-day sense, you'll be all right. As you get older, this will become increasingly important so, again, set up your life-habits now.

The most important factors in your exercise programme are that you should enjoy it, and that it should suit your age, body-type and fitness level. At your age, your body is going through many physical and hormonal changes so your exercise programme needs to be adaptable and should take into account the fact that you haven't finished growing.

If you are overweight, see a doctor to determine why, look closely at your diet and increase your exercise levels for a while.

Preventing ill-health

Good health is much more than not getting sick. It is an attitude of mind, the way your body feels, an enjoyment of living. Even if you never get 'flu or a cold or injuries, if you drag yourself out of bed every day feeling unenthusiastic and lethargic, I don't think you could say you were a healthy person. All your physical functions need to be working well; for example, if you get regular stomach upsets or headaches, or suffer from chronic constipation, insomnia or depression, your body is telling you that something is out of balance. For insomnia, see the next section of this chapter; for depression, see chapter 8. For constipation and other related conditions, check your diet to ensure that you're eating enough roughage (fibre); make sure you get adequate exercise; and give yourself plenty of time to use the toilet, as many bad habits can be set up by hurrying.

I had a chronic bladder condition which continued into my teenage years and caused me a lot of anguish. It was caused by an incident when I was a child and got locked in a toilet by mistake. This fear prevented me from developing healthy and normal urinary elimination. I either didn't go at all or I went very seldom, resulting in fluid retention and eventual infection. I even used to have bad dreams of ugly, dirty toilets that I couldn't use. It took me many years and professional help to come to understand this problem, and about ten years ago, I finally released it. If you are suffering from anything like this, don't be ashamed to ask for help as you don't need to suffer for years as I did.

Good health is not the same as fitness. Good health is the absence of disease; fitness is to do with the efficiency of the body, stamina, breathing capacity, heart function, and so on. Ideally, we should strive for both, but keep in mind that too much absorption in sport and exercise is just as undesirable as neglect of physical fitness. Remember what we found in the section on addiction — too much concentration on anything is unhealthy and can become obsessive.

There's no need to punish the body in order to get results. Start slowly on any programme you decide to take up. While a competitive spirit is fine, as is wanting to win, if that becomes the be-all and end-all, you've lost sight of the original purpose for getting involved. Keep things in perspective and don't let anyone push you unduly.

We get sick when we allow ourselves to become run down, and that relates back to stress again. Stress reduces the efficiency of the body's immune system; two people could be in a room with a virus or infection and only the stressed, tired, unbalanced one will get sick. Stress can show itself in many different ways. It can manifest as an actual attack similar to heart trouble, with chest pains and shortness of breath. But it can also be present in excessive amounts without showing up in any obvious way until the person 'breaks down' one day or finds that certain areas of life, such as work or health, are gradually disintegrating.

Because of excessive stress, I had a lifetime of being sick until ten years ago when I decided I'd had enough. I took control of my own health by changing my attitudes and lifestyle and I've never looked back. Don't let anyone talk you into believing that you are 'sickly', because that sort of thinking will keep you in bed and prevent you from enjoying life to the full. You can get out there and enjoy everything when you learn to balance your spiritual, emotional, physical and intellectual processes. It's not as hard as it sounds. One of my favourite sayings is, 'There is no way to happiness. Happiness is the way.' It might sound simplistic but if you're happy, things go right. More of this in chapter 8.

Insomnia

Sleep is one of nature's great gifts and is wonderful and healing. Here is something that you can use to cure emotional problems. We even have a common saying in our culture, 'sleep on it', when we have a problem that we're grappling with or a difficult decision to make. The secret is to get the right amount of sleep, not too much or too little. You can't catch up so there's no use in having ten hours one night and three the next. You need balance in this area as in diet and exercise. When things get hectic and you're under pressure, don't cut back on eating and sleeping regularly as you'll feel worse, not better. I've heard horrific stories of teenagers going without sleep for days, surviving on coffee and cigarettes or, worse still, taking 'uppers' to stay awake for an exam or social event. Your body will fight back against that sort of abuse even if you get away with it in the short-term.

If you find it hard to sleep properly, there are a number of possible reasons. Insomnia is a common stress symptom, as we saw at the beginning of the book. You could be over-anxious, or have poor sleeping habits or other health problems that affect the natural process of sleep. Although sleeping is perfectly ordinary, you need to prepare mentally for it. Sometimes, you can just fall into bed and straight to sleep, but many nights, you're either over-tired or not sleepy enough, and then your brain starts working overtime, going over all the events of the day and the things you want to do tomorrow. Once this happens, it's harder and harder to relax and go to sleep. Then time's ticking on and you start getting anxious about how many hours you're going to get before that alarm goes off. Anxiety affects most human endeavours and sleep is no exception. If you feel yourself getting anxious in bed when you're trying to doze off, do some deep breathing or relaxation exercises to unwind. It's better to do that before you get into bed, either by reading for a short while or watching some television or having a hot drink. Avoid stimulation just prior to bed, for example, no lively conversations or loud rock music! A soothing meditation or very light exercise is helpful just before jumping into bed.

If, having done all that, you still find yourself lying there wide awake, you'd be better off turning the light on and getting up for a while than lying in the dark, growing more and more anxious. Learn to turn your brain off at the end of the day. Nothing is ever solved by worry, and everything seems bleaker at night, so let go and start life's battles again in the morning.

Tanning

I can't leave this chapter without touching on a subject that, again, has been hammered by the media in recent years, but in case you're not convinced, I feel it's an important inclusion in a chapter on health. It's about sun tanning. The sun is wonderful. It warms the earth, helps things to grow, lights the day, is, in fact, life-giving, but it's a case of 'too much of a good thing' if you allow yourself to get burnt or spend too long in the sun working on a tan.

When I was a teenager, it was the 'done thing' to spend hours every day in summer getting brown. I was lucky to have the type of skin that tans easily but I still got burnt many times during my teenage years. Up till a few years ago, I still worked on a tan each summer, but now I never lie out in the sun on a really hot day and I still get brown by just walking around and working outdoors in the sunshine. I find that if I'm careful, especially at the start of summer, I never get burnt. It's a case of moderation, lots of sunscreen, and a large hat if you're out during the hottest part of the day. As long as a tan remains fashionable, teenagers will continue to sunbake, so, as with all the other things discussed in this book, just be cautious and remember, prevention is better than cure.

Here's a cautionary tale: A young woman with very fair skin and light hair found a lump on the back of her leg which turned out to be a malignant melanoma. It had to be cut away with a lot of surrounding flesh, and that patient now cannot ever go into the sun with her skin exposed. The cancer had been caused by prolonged sun damage over many years. Luckily, the cancer was caught in time and this person survived. Many Australians are not so lucky.

7 Work and Employment

So far, most of the stresses we've looked at have been in relation to home and school life and to the emotions. Many of you will have left school and your families and are out in the world trying to make a living and a future for yourselves, especially if you're at the older end of the teenage spectrum. In this chapter, we will examine work in its wider meaning, job-seeking and money, all subjects that are of vital interest if you're out in the workforce or hoping to be.

Career choices

Most of you have been giving some thought to your future goals and directions ever since you entered high school. If you're a teenager who knows exactly what job you want to attain or what career path you hope to follow, you're relatively lucky because indecision is the thief of time and success. Without a clear idea, you're liable to drift through your school days right up to leaving at Year 10, 11 or 12. By doing this, you make yourself vulnerable to failure and disappointment as you have few skills and no experience to offer prospective employers.

It is not the hirer's responsibility to consider you in the most favourable light or agree to train you. You have to develop as many desirable features as possible, build up your resumé so that you look attractive as an employment prospect, sell yourself, and convince the interviewer you can do the job. None of this is easy, and I will go through these points with you one by one in the course of this chapter.

Try firstly to narrow down your options. If you truly have no burning desire or ambition, write a 'wish' list: list down all the jobs you'd like if you had a magic wand and could just pick and choose. That gives you a starting point. Then, write down a list of your main talents and assets. You may be low on experience but high on enthusiasm, natural ability and energy, all valuable assets. Try to broaden your thinking. What you might consider no big deal could be very desirable to an employer. Think of such things as: good with your hands, fast thinker, good concentration, interested in a wide variety of topics, and so on.

Next, go to the library and scour through books and journals about career choices, interview selection processes, the requirements for various occupations and application procedures. The more knowledge you have at your fingertips, the sharper your competitive edge. TAFE colleges offer a counselling service which includes career aptitude testing and advice on your best choice of action, whether it's applying for a job straight away, taking some technical courses or learning some specific skills for a career you're interested in. If you have academic ability, you will no doubt apply for a place at a university or a college of advanced education, and if you're successful, you will spend three or four more years studying towards your chosen career.

Once you have a plan, you can set about to make it happen. Everything in life should be tackled in stages so that your goals and the strategies to achieve them always stay clear. If you're lucky enough to have supportive parents who encourage you and are prepared to keep you until you can earn your own living, you have the luxury of time and choice. If you don't get along with your family and move out of home when you leave school, you will have a greater struggle but more freedom and independence, so it's six of one and half a dozen of the other. There are government grants to apply for if you want to study further, or you can get unemployment benefit until you find paid work.

Work

The word 'work' covers a lot of ground and means different things to different people. As a word, it simply means labour, effort, but its social meaning takes in a lot more than that. To some, work means no more than putting in eight hours somewhere and getting paid for it; to others, it's tied up with ego and personal achievement — what is work to one person might be pleasure to another. A good example of this is, say, gardening. A professional gardener might call planting, weeding and watering 'work', yet to the person who simply loves a home garden these activities could spell pleasure.

It is said that the wise person finds a way to make a loved hobby or interest earn money so that work and pleasure are one. That makes sense to me. As a teacher, writer, speaker and counsellor, I can honestly say I love all my jobs and would do them whether I was paid or not.

Of course, most of us have to face the reality of making a living, so it would be great if you could decide what you like best and find a way to make it pay. We can't all be actors, pilots and clowns, but try to tap into your own personal pleasures, things that give you a real buzz in life, and find corresponding jobs. For example, if you love cars and mechanical things, try to get work in a garage; if you love reading, train as a librarian or a literature teacher. The possibilities are only limited by your imagination and energy.

Keep in mind that you control your own destiny. Don't wait for others to prop you up or lead you along. Decide what you want and go for it. Knowing, deciding and a plan of attack are your best tools. Most of you will work most of your lives. Don't make the mistake of jumping into the first job offering, hating it and feeling stuck, or, alternatively, giving up on your future because you get discouraged or fail at your first few attempts.

Work can be one of the most satisfying areas of your life, and I feel that you'd be cheating yourself if you believed otherwise. So many people are cynical about work and jobs, striving only to get the best holidays, wages and conditions for themselves, never trying to give anything back to the employer or doing extra hours in order to help the organisation they work for. This is a very limited view of work, and unlikely to bring much joy in the long-term. If you have to spend a third of your life at a place of employment, wouldn't you rather it be enjoyable if at all possible? All jobs, even the most varied and interesting, have an element of drudgery and tedium attached to them, but your attitude is going to be the deciding factor.

Jobs that allow room for your creative input, initiative and ideas are ideal. Not all of you will find this, nor may you all desire it. Decide what's right for you, not just for the immediate future, but for the years to come. If you're not sure, you'd be better to take casual work and keep looking around.

Case study. A man in his thirties consulted me because he felt very dissatisfied in his work. He had a secure public service job, but he'd been in it since he left school and he now felt locked in with responsibilities, a wife and family, mortgage, etc. His true interest lay in writing but he couldn't see himself becoming a professional author under the circumstances. My advice to him was to explore the possibilities of part-time writing so he could still keep his job; he could write in his spare time, do courses and apply for grants once he got something published. Very few writers can afford to work at it full-time, but he could send stories or poems to magazines and newspapers and try to get support from a publisher if he had a saleable idea for a book.

This is just one example but there are probably millions of people who are in the wrong jobs or very unhappy with their employment. In our current economic climate one could say they're lucky to have any work, but that's no consolation to the individual. Perhaps as a race of people we would suffer less, economically and physically, if we enjoyed work more. Don't become just another statistic in this area. Dare to want more for yourself and strive for excellence in all you do. The best cure for boredom is to keep learning, to be interested in everything, and to feel satisfied that you've given your best every day.

Workaholism

This is unlikely to affect you greatly at your age but, if you have the sort of personality that is prone to perfectionism and if you tend to be very hard on yourself, you may develop into a workaholic. This is just another addiction and, as with alcohol, stress, drugs, etc., sufferers are in the control of an outside force, and in its power. In simple terms, work takes on an overly significant role and workaholics eventually live for nothing else. They can become very successful and financially well off but live in a very unbalanced way. Other areas of life, particularly personal ones, become severely neglected. The only 'cure' usually is a rude shock that makes the workaholic realise what's happening, such as a health scare or relationship breakdown. Even as a student at school or university, you will be aware if you have a tendency to push yourself too hard, give yourself too heavy a workload and expect unreasonable results, so just watch this as you get older and the pressures around you increase.

Self-employment

Some of you will opt for self-employment, which can range from cleaning car windows at traffic lights to running a multi-million-dollar corporation. All it means is that you are your own boss and take responsibility for your own income, work conditions, future security, etc. It's not for everyone as most people would prefer to be sure of a regular pay packet, but if you are the independent type and are prepared to take risks, this may be suitable for you a bit down the track. I certainly wouldn't recommend that a school-leaver try self-employment before experiencing employment in general.

There are government initiatives that seek to help young people to enter small business, offering funding, advice and back-up services, but there's a lot more to self-employment than just the freedom of being your own boss. You need to be prepared to work for as many hours as a job takes — there are no paid breaks or annual holidays. You have to be able to do everything, not just the work you like; for example, you'll need to take care of insurance, tax, staffing, accounting and administrative matters. You have to be self-motivating. There'll be no-one there to pat you on the back for a job well done. There's no getting fed-up and tired. Every day, you'll have to get up and face the same battles, and even when you win, it's only a temporary victory. You have to create your own income, day after day, week after week. If you're the boss, you're responsible for all expenses, and the money has to be found one way or the other, so you have very little security or peace of mind.

I hope I've convinced you that it takes a special type of person to enjoy self-employment and make it work. I tried it for six years and really hated it. It taught me a lot and I have no regrets, but I'd say learn a lot more about yourself, life, work and finances before seriously contemplating a life of self-employment.

Preparing for employment

Okay, you've done your research and you know what you want to do, career-wise. What happens now? As I said before, if you're tertiary studies material, you'd know it by school-leaving; if you want to enter a trade, you can apply for an apprenticeship or take technical courses. For specific career information, check with your school guidance counsellor, TAFE vocational counselling or a reference library.

But what if you want to take a job straight away? It's still best to have an area of work in mind, and then plan your course of action. Places to look for work include: newspaper advertisements, noticeboards at local shopping centres, libraries, newsagents, etc., job boards at your local employment office. Don't be afraid to let people know you're looking for work as you can pick up leads and contacts by chance.

However, a more direct approach could work best. Rather than waiting for jobs to be advertised or to come to your attention, why not write letters of enquiry to places where you'd like to work? If you decide to try this, ensure that you know something about the company and that you have at least some basic ability to offer them; for example, there's no point applying to a shoe factory if your only experience is working with cars! Employers often admire initiative in applicants and might consider interviewing you rather than advertising a position. Even if there's nothing available immediately, you might be placed on a waiting list and contacted for employment later.

Applying for a job

When it comes to applying, you have two main methods to choose from. Sometimes, advertisements ask applicants to just show up but that's rare, and I wouldn't recommend you try the personal approach unless it's for casual work like helping in a shop or household help. The two methods are written and phone applications.

Phone applications

These are difficult, as you have to get your message across

without the benefit of any visual input. This is what you need to do:
- Write down what you want to say before you dial.
- Have intelligent questions about the job ready at hand, even though you may not get the chance to ask them.
- Speak clearly and confidently, even if you're very nervous.
- If you're asked to attend an interview, find out what you need to bring with you, for example, documents or certificates, resumé, references, written evidence of skills or experience, or anything else required.
- Be very polite as, if you impress the person on the phone, you'll smooth the path for the interview.
- Don't be discouraged if you're not asked to come in straight away — sometimes, companies like to compile a list of interested applicants and narrow them down before interviewing.

Written applications

Written applications are easier insofar as you can take your time and plan out what you want to say. Nowadays, resumés are expected even for relatively simple jobs, whereas once only professional positions required them. There are secretarial and employment services which will prepare a very nice-looking resumé for you to take to interviews and send out with applications, but this might be too expensive for you. Your local CES can help you with this, or you could ask your parents, relatives or friends if they have any expertise in this area. You just need some guidance.

Here are some pointers to good resumé writing:
- On the front page, list all the facts about yourself: name, address, phone number, age, then the job you're applying for in bold type.
- Have a page for each area of information you want to offer.
- Typed pages are better but, if you must write, ensure that your information is set out clearly and neatly.
- Don't worry if you haven't had any jobs as you can include details of clubs you belong to, medals or awards you've

received, any volunteer work you've done, seminars or workshops you've attended; also, reports from teachers or supervisors are very helpful.
- Think of your resumé as a selling document — put down anything and everything you can think of to enhance your chances. That's what will decide the hirer about calling you in for an interview or passing you over.
- Never write down anything you can't back up, but it's quite legitimate to include any activity that could add to your suitability for the job.
- These are the headings you should include:
  NAME
  ADDRESS
  DATE OF BIRTH
  MARITAL STATUS
  QUALIFICATIONS/EDUCATION HISTORY
  EMPLOYMENT HISTORY AND/OR OTHER RELEVANT EXPERIENCE
  MARKETABLE SKILLS
  INTERESTS/HOBBIES
  PERSONAL ATTRIBUTES (for example, adaptable, good speaker)

With the resumé, you need only include a basic letter of application, stating your interest in the position and why you think you are a suitable candidate.

If you absolutely cannot compile a resumé, your letter of application will need to be more detailed but don't overload it with information. Again, neatness and clarity are key requirements.

The interview

If you get as far as the interview, it means that you have a real chance at the job. Here are the main points to remember when going to a job interview:
- Dress neatly and suitably

- Punctuality is absolutely essential
- Try for a confident but polite manner
- Be prepared with relevant questions
- Answer the interviewer honestly; if you don't have certain information, just say so.
- Don't be afraid to check details about pay rates and hours of work — employers admire initiative as long as it's within the bounds of good taste.
- Ask when you can expect to hear the result of your interview. These days, sometimes only the successful candidate is notified. It's better to know this before you leave so that you don't spend the next two weeks waiting for a verdict that never comes.
- Avoid trying to be 'clever' as employers prefer applicants to show a willingness to learn, especially if you are applying for an unskilled position.
- Your body language says a lot about you. You give out signals with every movement, gesture and body position, by the way you speak, move, walk into a room, hold your head, give eye contact, interact with others. There's no way to disguise your attitudes, feelings and thoughts unless you're consciously putting on an act. If you lack confidence, it will appear in your body language so be very aware of this when you attend job interviews. There's no need to be overly selfconscious, but quiet attention to your non-verbal communication is useful.

I won't try to kid you: it is very demoralising to be unsuccessful in applying for a job. With each 'failure', it's harder to write that next letter, attend that next interview. So, how do you overcome this hurdle? You apply for lots of jobs so that you don't put all your eggs into one basket. You take advantage of every opportunity that presents itself without counting on each one to be the ultimate. You go into the interview with optimism and confidence, giving it your best shot, yet at the same time realising that you may simply not be the best applicant for the job and it's no reflection on you personally if you're not chosen.

These attitudes require maturity and a healthy self-esteem, hard qualities to muster even for a teenager who feels successful, let alone if you're feeling down on yourself and on life in general. So, let's look at the unemployment issue which affects each one of us at some time in our lives.

Unemployment

Unemployment is simply the state of being out of work, but unfortunately it has much stronger implications to the individual and to the community. Our society revolves around material success and status: what you have, who you are and what you own. Roles within this framework are played out every day, and one of the key roles that any individual plays is the occupational one. The second question that we're usually asked when we're out socially, after our names, is 'What do you do for a living?' When you were still at school, your identity was caught up with your parents', but as soon as you become 'marketable' the pressure is on from friends, relatives, neighbours and even perfect strangers to get you employed and settled. If you ever get the chance, see a film called *The Graduate*. The character that Dustin Hoffman plays is hassled from all sides as soon as he graduates and the film explores his choices and how he finally breaks free.

There is usually a period of grace after school-leaving, and if you have a definite plan and understanding parents, everything will probably hang loose for a while. It's only when the weeks stretch into months, and the interviews can be counted in hundreds instead of dozens, that the pressure mounts. It's asking a lot for you to stay positive under these conditions, but in the next chapter, you'll see how important and even essential it is to do this if you are to succeed.

Here are some tips on banishing the unemployment blues:
- Firstly, get out from behind any labels like 'dole-bludger' or 'parasite'. If you are genuinely trying to get work, you have no reason to believe negative things about yourself.

- Keep busy, not just to fill in the days but for self-esteem.
- Volunteer for unpaid work if that's all that's offering for now — this can sometimes lead to a paid job.
- Make one attempt at least every day towards getting work as you can fall into lazy habits very easily.
- Keep mentally and physically fit.
- Don't allow yourself to get stressed out looking for work — even unemployed people have a right to leisure and a social life.
- Try to maintain a balance in your everyday activities. Don't over-focus on jobs, jobs, jobs.
- Practise stress management as no-one is going to hire you if you're obviously strung out, unfit or tense.

Success

Success isn't just getting what we want in life. It's an attitude of mind. If you believe yourself to be successful, you are. No-one can take that away from you. Of course, once you get into a job, you have to be successful in the boss's eyes and that's a little more difficult.

Right from the outset, it's important to turn up on time every day, attend diligently to your assigned duties without shortcuts or carelessness, be polite and obliging to your superiors, and try to fulfil all your tasks with enthusiasm, even the tedious ones. However, as you will no doubt be starting at the bottom of the ladder in the company, you could have to put up with more than your share of unpleasant jobs, bossy supervisors and extra duties. That's just the way it works and we've all been through it. If the job you get has a future, stick out this initial phase, thinking of it as a learning period. If it's a dead-end job or just a casual stop-gap, keep looking out in your own time for something with better prospects.

However unimportant the job may be in your long-term plan, do it well because you need to build up your resume and get good references. One of the most undesirable features on an employment record is a string of short-term jobs, so don't leave on a whim. Each job, though minor in itself, is a stepping stone to your future dream. Never, never be afraid to dream, for if you lose that ability your life will always be a struggle and even your successes unfulfilling.

No matter how long it takes you to realise your life's dream, hold on tight to it, adapt it as you go through the years, let it go in times of discouragement or complacency, but keep coming back to it, and believe in it because it belongs to you alone. There'll always be plenty of people to tell you it's impossible and a load of rubbish but don't let them put you off.

Some people are afraid of failure and some of success. When you're applying for jobs, you're nervous and afraid of rejection. That's perfectly understandable. However, I've been told by teenagers that after months and months of job hunting, another fear creeps in. It takes the form of thinking 'But can I cut it if I get the job?' If this becomes severe enough, you might sabotage your own efforts, work against yourself, and actually stop yourself succeeding. So, be careful of this trap.

Money

Handling money is a skill you need all your life. From the time you had a small school bank account and put your pocket money in it each week, you realised that it takes cash to get many of the things you want. Saving or spending — this is the dilemma that faces all of us. Resolving this conflict is not so important when you're a child, it's more vital as you get into your teen years, and it becomes crucial when you start earning your own money, especially if you leave home and have to support yourself. Budgeting is sensible for everyone at whatever age, but as a teenager you're unlikely to be earning a high income so keep money management very simple. Here are some basic tips:

- For tax purposes, save all your income records and receipts in a safe place, and get some advice before you fill in your first tax return.
- Pay your regular bills, or board if you're still at home, as soon as you get paid.
- Decide how much you can realistically afford to put aside every week out of your pay packet, and keep to it. It's almost better to commit to less and do it without fail than to a large amount you grudge and end up not banking.
- It's also important to allow yourself some 'play' money every week. If you're only working to pay bills and save, life can become very dull and the whole point of working is lost.
- Set clear goals for yourself as to what you want out of working. Are you saving towards a set goal like a car or holiday? Or do you just want to get some savings behind you? It's important to give yourself incentives in order to achieve your target, whatever it is. For example, if you can enjoy some small rewards along the way, this will keep you motivated towards your bigger goals.

Your attitude to money will vary and change throughout your life. Right now, it's probably just a means to an end. You want to buy things and you need money to do it. Later, money will begin to represent many other ideas to you. Our society worships money, so having it endows power and status. If these goals are important to you, by all means pursue money with them in mind.

Money means different things to different people. Some want to accumulate it as a way to have security; others want to use it to acquire more possessions; yet others see it as granting freedom. Almost all of us want more money than we need just for the necessities in life so that we can buy some luxuries, travel, have nice homes and cars, look after our families, and so on. The idea of winning a lot of money in a lottery is the favourite fantasy of many people. Sure, I buy my weekly Lotto ticket along with millions of other Australians but I understand that if I ever did win, it would not be simply joyful; sudden wealth is a complex business and many winners have lived to regret their 'luck'. There's a good saying: 'If you want to be happy for a year, win the lottery; if you want to be happy for the rest of your life, find work you love'.

I'm not trying to dissuade you from wishing to be rich, but be clear on your motivations about money. Don't let money be the way in which you try to solve all of life's problems. Find security within yourself first and then acquire money. While you're waiting to win it, work hard, save a little, buy a house and find out about some modest investments. Very few of us are destined for enormous wealth and many who achieve it, lose it.

My philosophy about money is that you should use it for your needs and not be overly concerned about how much you have. Enjoy it and don't let it dictate your attitude towards yourself or others. I have made the mistake of judging my own worth by how much money I had or didn't have. I had to learn the hard way that I am rich in a thousand ways that have nothing whatever to do with money. You know the expression, 'The best things in life are free.' Well, money certainly can buy many wonderful things but we all own the oceans and the trees and the sunsets and the flowers; if we would only stop to appreciate them more often, and participate in saving our planet from further destruction, we would be wealthy indeed.

Goals and motivation

Without being too rigid about it, it's good to have goals in life. Some people have one-year, five-year and ten-year plans but you don't need to go that far at your age. I think a month-to-month plan is plenty, with a rough idea of where you want to be in a year's time. This applies to financial matters as well as personal and career.

Here are some general points about goal-setting:

Goals and Goal setting

- Keep the goals realistic
- Keep them small
- Give self rewards
- Write them down
- Be specific
- Have short and long term goals

What is motivation? Simply put, it is enthusiasm, energy and keenness, all essential to get any enterprise off the ground and make it work. There's hardly anything you could make successful without the motivation to start it, maintain it and conclude it, whether it's job-seeking, getting fit, saving money, having good relationships or finding personal happiness. It's easier to see it working in concrete examples but motivation is needed in all areas of life.

In the next chapter, I will examine some less practical but equally important strategies you can use to reduce stress levels in your life and increase your personal happiness and success.

8 Personal Growth

In this chapter, my aim is to explore with you some of the less practical, but equally important, aspects of personal development. Up till now, we have discussed all the many things in life that can cause you stress, and what you can do to reduce and manage it better. But prevention is preferable, and if you can learn as teenagers to think and behave more positively, your road ahead will be much smoother and clearer.

There is too much emphasis these days on doom and gloom: unemployment, poverty, homelessness, the recession, the environment, world strife — the list goes on and on. I'm not suggesting for a moment that these are not important issues, and, as young people coming into an age of responsibility and power, you need to know where you stand on social and world affairs so that you can do your part.

My argument is that it's difficult to imagine changing the world if you have a negative attitude to life and all it offers. Identify the areas that need improvement, by all means, but don't get bogged down in cynicism and pessimism. There are plenty of adults around who will supply you with heaps of negative and limited thoughts. In this chapter, I hope to redress that balance and offer you the flip side. Even if you take notice of 10 per cent of what I say, you'll hopefully achieve more, enjoy life and be less stressed!

Religion

Many of you will have grown up in families where religion plays a major part. As teenagers, a healthy scepticism is to be expected. If you still believe in God, attend church services regularly and value your spiritual life, you're probably in the minority but also very lucky, if your religious beliefs are a source of strength for you. It's lovely to see a whole family at church together. With the disintegration of so much family life, group outings of any kind are not as common any more. Religion has a community face and a private one; the important thing is what you feel in your heart. There is little satisfaction in putting on a pious face if you don't feel it within. At your age, you should be able to make decisions for yourself regarding your future habits of worship, your religious and social values, and whether or not you accept the faith your family follows.

This is a source of tremendous stress and conflict within families because your parents naturally dislike you questioning beliefs and traditions that are so precious to them. Use tact. Question with common sense and reason, not argument and anger. When you leave home you'll be able to please yourself, so there's no need to create an emotional wrangle over an issue that rarely attracts total agreement anyway. You know what they say about never arguing over religion and politics — there's a good reason for that!

When I was growing up, I was extremely religious in the traditional sense. My family is Catholic and I embraced all the tenets of the church that I was taught at school and at home. Some of the contradictions in the teachings bothered me even when I was small, but the love of God and the joy of the ceremonies filled a hunger in me. It took many, many years into my adult life before I decided that a religious way of life was not for me. I am very grateful for the values I was taught and for the education I got from the nuns but, eventually, I had to follow my own conscience. I still believe in God but no longer accept any form of manmade religion.

In particular, I am wary of people who praise themselves as Christians, for true goodness is to be found in the heart and not on the lips.

This is a very personal decision for you, and I can only tell you of my own experience. Let your inner self guide you and you won't go wrong.

Spiritual life

Being spiritual is every human being's inheritance. It's not the same as being religious. You have a spiritual dimension whether you accept it or not. It's not within the scope of this book to talk extensively about metaphysics and philosophy, but I hope that you'll read up on these yourself in future years and expand your understanding of who you are. I always think it's sad when people say they believe we are only made up of a physical dimension, as that denies so much of what is mysterious and wonderful about human existence. Even traditional religion teaches that we have an eternal soul which continues after death; thus, spiritual life is everlasting.

Many metaphysical subjects such as astrology, numerology, clairvoyance, crystal healing, palmistry, etc., can easily be dismissed as hocus-pocus but they have some validity if studied seriously. At worst, they can be employed by dishonest practitioners to exploit those hungry for answers; at best, they offer help and guidance to the fuller enjoyment and understanding of life.

Many of you are probably already questioning the 'meaning of life'. Surely we can't just be meant to eat, sleep, work and then, one day, die? If we have a spiritual nature, how do we get in touch with it? Obviously, religious practices are one route, but many religions that don't come under the banner of 'traditional' can be studied and explored. Eastern philosophies, for example, have a lot to teach us, as they open our minds to other possibilities. My attitude to most things is have a close look before rejecting them. Scepticism borne of ignorance is worthless.

As with many of the issues discussed in the book so far, I suggest that you open your minds to learning in this area, not just book-learning but life-learning. See each day as an opportunity to add to your store of knowledge, and discard as you go along, the ideas that you don't feel are right for you. In this way, you are claiming the right to be in charge of your own mind, thoughts and choices. (Refer also to the section on identity in chapter 2.)

Your spiritual nature can be explored by things of beauty — music, nature and poetry, for instance. Creative pursuits can also be spiritual experiences. Some of you no doubt like to write or play musical instruments or paint. Even physical exercise can have a spiritual dimension if it's undertaken in the right frame of mind. Walking by water or swimming in a beautiful bay are wonderful ways to commune with the Creator, whatever you perceive him to be. If you see God as a wise old man in the sky with a white beard, that's who he is for you. I find God in the trees and the flowers and the sea and the wind; also in an empty church, and in homes where there is love, and in hospitals where people are suffering with great courage, and in schools and colleges where there is joyful learning. In other words, I find God wherever there is love and joy in the world. Humans create all the suffering and trouble in the world, not God, and we can't ask him to put everything right. We need to be responsible for ourselves and ask for help and guidance, but not sit back and expect God to give us everything without any effort on our part.

If you can recognise your spiritual nature and nurture it every day, you will find a joy in life that goes beyond physical pleasures or worldly achievements.

Meditation and prayer are two effective ways to feed your spiritual needs, but these can take many forms. You are 'praying' when you help someone in need and you can 'meditate' on a beautiful painting. The main criterion is that your mind should be clear of practical concerns and mundane thoughts. Let your mind be at rest for short periods each day. At your age, your mind is running along at such high speeds that it's good to just stop and catch up with yourself from time to time. If you can fit a short period of solitude into your daily routine, that's the ideal but, if not, take 'time out' as often as you can.

Affirmations

These are a modern form of prayer, and they work very well if you have the right attitude about them and are prepared to wait for results. It's pretty sad if you only pray when you want something. Prayer is much more satisfying if it's part of your daily life. This is what I do: Each morning, I give thanks for a new day and all the blessings of my life. I send good thoughts out to all my family and friends, to all the animals of the world, and to all the places I'm going to that day, and I place a protective shield over my home and possessions. Each night, I let go of all the day's problems, disappointments, hurts and grudges. This is an especially important thing to do so that you don't wake each day with the weight of yesterday's pain — remember what we talked about in chapter 6 regarding the link between emotional stress and poor health. I also affirm that I sleep well and wake refreshed, and I ask my dream guide to walk with me during my night's adventures. We all have spirit guides or guardians who watch over us through our journey in life, and you can ask them to help you and keep you safe.

So, what are affirmations? They're statements of clear intent that you can say out loud or inwardly. Every day of your lives, you are programmed to believe things that others want you to; affirmations are simply a way to put into your mind ideas you want to have about yourself, life, money, success, anything at all.

Before you start each day, you can say to yourself such statements as:
- I am an energetic and successful person.
- Today, I bring good things into my life.
- I always have terrific relationships.

These are just examples, but the same principle can be used for specific areas of life that you want to work on, such as an exam you have to sit, or a difficult relationship you're grappling with, or a health problem. For affirmations to work, you need to state them clearly, always in the present tense, and use 'I'. You can't affirm things for anyone else; for example, if you've been fighting with someone, it won't work if you say 'Mary changes her attitude towards me', but it might work if you say, 'Today, I understand Mary better', or 'I am more patient with Mary today'.

You can change affirmations as they become redundant. Write your own. That way, they'll be more meaningful for you. At first, they'll seem mechanical and pointless, but if you keep saying the ones you want to really work, they'll start to change your thinking and therefore your life. I began working with affirmations six years ago, and only a few months back, came to realise that I was truly living some of the ones I've been saying all this time. As you get older, I'm sure you will see the value in this type of re-programming. Firstly, you need to understand the tremendous power in your mind that is largely untapped.

Mind power

If you thought you had a huge reserve of oil under the earth in your backyard, wouldn't you want to dig down and pump it out? Well, that's what it's like with mind power. Many people live and die without realising the capabilities they have. I'm not just talking about intelligence or talent but the ability of the mind to shape your thoughts and feelings. This is something that all human beings can do, regardless of education or IQ. That's why it's so important that you don't think negatively any more than you can help. It almost seems as if it's in human nature to be negative. Once you're aware of it, try to keep replacing your negative thoughts with positive. Every time you catch yourself out, quite consciously and deliberately change your thinking. Here's an example: 'I'm not going to get chosen for the school band' could become 'I'm going to try really hard to get into the school band'. What about 'No-one likes me' becoming the affirmation 'I am the type of person people like'? I hope you get the idea.

There's not room here to tell you about all these matters in detail, but if you write to me direct, I'll recommend further reading for you and tell you more about the methods that have helped me. For now, just keep in mind that you have the choice of how you think, feel and behave. If you start the day with negative thinking, there's a strong chance that you'll live out your expectations and have a 'bad' day. This is called a self-fulfilling prophecy, a set of circumstances that occurs as a direct result of beliefs about it. The best example I can offer is in the field of sport, where psychology is used extensively to achieve winning results. Athletes who really want to win have firstly to believe in that outcome. No-one ever wins by thinking negative thoughts or by having wishy-washy ambitions. 'If I win, fine, if I don't, who cares' will not get you past the winning post. At the same time, investing totally in a set outcome can bring a lot of heartache and disappointment. After all, all efforts take time to ferment and come to maturity. If we could all just step up to the diving board, the stage or the podium and be champions straight-away, where would be the challenge?

This may sound like a contradiction but, actually, it's about our old friend balance again. 'Planning for success while accepting the challenge' is the best way I can put it. But it all starts in your mind. Anything you don't like about yourself can be changed by changing how you think. Your thoughts also directly affect the way you feel, so depression, anxiety, boredom and unhappiness can all be traced back to negative thinking.

Positive thinking

This is a much overused and misused term. What it doesn't mean is that you have to be smiling and happy all the time. It's more an attitude of mind than a state of the emotions. As we saw earlier, what you think eventually gets translated into how you feel, so there is a definite connection between the two.

Positive thinking is about how you perceive the difficulties and challenges in your life. Do you throw in the towel at the first obstacle? Do you always look at the dark side in situations or try to find a 'silver lining'? Do you allow yourself to think negatively most of the time? These are good questions to ask yourself in order to find out where you stand. By nature, some of you will be more optimistic and cheerful but positive thinking is possible for all types of people. I believe it is one of the best tools you can possess in life, and one you're at the perfect age to learn and practise.

We saw in the last chapter how important a positive attitude is in job seeking and attaining career success. However, it doesn't end there. Choosing a positive approach over a negative one becomes second nature; then hurdles, no matter how real, are all conquerable.

Think of it as running a race. If you think of the running itself, the strain and pain of every step and mile, you won't even start. Think instead of the end of the race, the result rather than the effort. This can apply to many areas of your daily life. If you're job-seeking, see yourself in the job you want; don't concentrate on the trail of interviews and unpleasant experiences you've got to go through to get there. See yourself passing that exam, getting that boy or girl to notice you, losing weight, improving your family life, whatever you want. Positive thinking is not the result of good things happening to you but rather the cause. The more positively you think and feel, the better life goes. It is a choice you have to make, and it takes real commitment. It's much easier to be negative. For a start, you'll have more company, and secondly, it takes less effort to feel sorry for yourself because of all the things that are wrong in your life. No life is free of problems. Thousands of times every day, you are pitted against obstacles, and you can fold or fight. It's up to you.

Here are some ideas to help you think more positively:

The Role of Positive Thinking

- Not unrealistic, false happiness; but an attitude, a way of life
- Happiness as an integral part of living, not a fixed goal
- How do I start thinking positively, after perhaps years of negative thinking?
- Replacing the negative with the positive
- Positive thinking linked directly to self-esteem and confidence
- The role of identity in positive thinking
- Mind power
- Don't control — reshape!
- Fear and doubt — our two worst enemies
- Fear is a fantasy
- Self-image and signals; body language
- The mind and disease
- Intuition and the 'inner you'

Creative visualisation

This is a fancy-sounding name for a relatively straightforward tool of positive thinking. If you break the two words down, it means to create (make out of nothing) pictures/images/visions, to visualise. Rather than just thinking vaguely about the things you want to bring into your life, imagine concrete images. Picture yourself in that office or shop or factory. See yourself with that desired date. What would you be wearing, doing, saying? Where are you? How did you get there? The more detail you visualise, the better it works. Use sights, sounds, smells, real images that you can conjure up and build on till the whole experience is real to you, not just wishful thinking. If you want something and your attitude is 'If I get it, fine, but I don't expect to really', of course you won't succeed. It's the same as with affirmations. They have to be said with conviction, until the belief in your mind becomes reality.

This may all sound like fairyland but it does work in a very tangible way if you put your heart into it. It's easy to see that negative thinking brings negative results, so why should we not believe that this principle works equally well in the realm of the positive? Try it. You have nothing to lose but your 'victim mentality'.

Inner peace

Living in a society, relationship skills and good communication are most necessary. Once you have done all the work outlined in this book — once you've reduced stress, learned more about yourself, improved your family life, become more positive, worked on your diet and fitness, and achieved career success — you still have the most important task ahead. You now need to find a way to be at peace with yourself and then reach out to others.

Perhaps 'peace' is an odd word to use in a book about teenagers. Peace has very little to do with conflict, rebellion and change. But I hope you will use the ideas in this book beyond your teenage years. Peace will become much more vital to you as you grow into your adult and mature years. How to achieve this is to learn about the world within you, your inner self. That voice inside that you may think of as your 'conscience', and that I prefer to call your intuition, is your best guide in good times and bad. Many people only call on this inner wisdom when they're in crisis. Why not use it every day as your best friend and helper? All you have to do is sit quietly, anytime, anywhere, to hear it. You don't 'hear' it in the physical sense, but ideas, solutions, insights come into your mind as you allow them. If you're busy rushing around all the time, you miss the many messages that your subconscious mind is trying to tell you, so make time to 'listen', and meditate upon what comes. If your mind is always noisy and chaotic, it's hard to know what's real and what isn't, what's important and what is trivial. It can take years, even a whole lifetime, to achieve this peace of mind, so don't get discouraged if it doesn't work when you try it. Even imperfect meditation will help you.

Personal power

We spoke earlier in the book about how powerless most children feel; even as teenagers you probably think that you are at the mercy of adults and authority figures in your life. To some extent, we are all answerable to other people — the government, organisations, and society in general. No-one can be totally free; that's a myth. What you can have is personal power, which is related to your sense of identity, the social roles you play and the strength of your inner life. Personal power is made up of the following elements:
- Integrity — living by your own truth and a set of moral codes
- Honesty — not only with others but with yourself
- Faith — religious or otherwise
- Morality — being clear about what is right and wrong, and making the correct choices
- Having personal values that you live and die by
- Having the courage to know yourself and be true to yourself

Sticking to what you believe in the face of opposition and ridicule is one of the most difficult things you'll ever be called on to do in life. Right from owning up when you've done the wrong thing in school, to paying your debts, to being a trustworthy friend, to accepting your responsibilities — these all require moral courage. But the 'near enough is good enough' school of thinking is still alive and well today, and many people believe it's the cause of Australia's current economic problems. If you are hard-working, loyal and caring, your friends and co-workers might rubbish you, call you a wowser or a snob. The same applies when you don't want to drink or gamble or join in petty crime, or if you have strong religious views. Most of you will not be put in situations where you'll be asked to make moral decisions on really big subjects; if you are, it will be once or twice in a lifetime. It's the little crossroads every day that will test you, for example, whether to tell that white lie, or to keep the change that was too much. Your parents, teachers and ministers can only point you in the right direction; the journey is yours alone.

Claiming your personal power takes high self-esteem, and a good deal of faith in yourself. In teenagers, this is sometimes called 'cheek' or 'nerve'. In an adult, these are highly prized qualities, so don't be put off by any criticism you might receive now. Always look within for answers when in doubt, and have enough faith to stick to your guns if you truly believe you are right. The solutions you get from the bottle, the cigarette and the drug will not sustain you. They are false and lead you away from your own true, beautiful self. If you can believe this one thing, you will have gained one of life's greatest secrets.

Already you will know that living in a society is like walking a tightrope. It's a balancing act between personal desires and beliefs against the good of the whole and conforming to mass opinion. You have to somehow do both, and it does get easier as you get older. Teenagers tend to see life in black and white terms: what you want against what you can get. Soon, this blurs into shades of grey as compromise becomes easier and you learn to settle for what you can have rather than try to force everything into your own personal mould.

That's not to say you shouldn't hold onto your dreams and fantasies, for what would life be without them? It's a case of knowing when to fight and when to give in, and only experience teaches you that particular lesson.

Communication

This is particularly difficult for teenagers as you tend to lack the confidence and social skills to do it well, especially with people out of your own age-group. That's why your friendships with peers are so important to you. But remember, communication can take many forms. There is the non-verbal variety we discussed in chapter 7; there's talking, gestures, touching, facial expression, formal discussion, debate, chit-chat, just to name a few. Making polite conversation with strangers, what is known as 'small talk', is tricky for most of us, and usually teenagers just don't even try. That's okay, as it's a skill that comes with practice.

Communication at deeper levels, however, is air and water to the teenager. There are so many things you want answers to, so much you want to talk over. Whoever you find to share this with, do it. It might be a loved teacher, a best friend or a group at school. This special kind of communication can only happen when there is mutual trust, honesty and a rapport between the two or more people.

As teenagers, you're probably more involved with your own pain and feelings than with understanding others, but, as you get older, reaching out to people who need your help and attention is very gratifying. It bridges the gap that exists between all people, especially those from different generations. I remember receiving a letter from a teenage boy who lived in an extended family. His concern was for his grandfather, who sat in an armchair all day, seemingly isolated from the rest of the family group. The boy was in conflict because, as much as he wanted to talk to his grandfather and share time with him, he also felt resentful of the restrictions placed on his activities by the old man's presence. He couldn't bring friends home or make a lot of noise. This story highlights a classic problem that often exists between people in different age-groups; the potential for misunderstanding is very great. A good deal of love and patience is required to reach communication, but the potential rewards are great.

Ageing and death

At your age, getting old and dying is very far from your mind, and I only introduce this subject because you live in a society where loved ones and strangers are old and dying around you. It is, therefore, important that you understand the issues surrounding a condition which affects every human being, sooner or later.

We talked about death earlier in the book and I said that it is an abstract until it happens to someone close to you. In the same way, ageing is a concept that you probably only think about in connection with your grandparents or the pensioner couple next door. What has it got to do with you personally? My belief is that we are all part of each other in a society, that your teenage problems cannot be separated from my adult concerns and those of all the different groups that inhabit our towns and cities, including our elder citizens. Indeed, they have a lot to teach us.

You may find yourself impatient or intolerant with their slower ways, rambling speech or hearing difficulties, but put yourself in their shoes and imagine how awful it is not to be listened to or respected any more. Take the time to help a senior citizen across the street or do something nice for your old neighbour; if you have the time, visit a retirement village or nursing home with joy and love to share — take your song and your smile and brighten someone else's day. You'll be amazed at how good it makes you feel. One of the best cures for stress is joining in a pleasant and generous interaction.

Death comes to all of us, but it's one of those subjects that people would rather not hear or talk about. The most frightening aspect of death is the fact that we know so little about it. Those who've had near-death experiences tell us that, after their spirits left their bodies, they saw a white light and felt very loved and protected. There has never been any report of fear or pain. That should give us some comfort. The manner of our dying is in the lap of the gods but I believe that our wishes have power. If you really want to die peacefully in your bed some day, hold onto that belief and let go of your doubt and fear.

As to life after death, your beliefs in this area will depend on your religious upbringing and your own thought processes. There are basically three choices: you just die and that's it; your soul/spirit leaves your body and goes to heaven or hell for reward or punishment; your soul has the choice of returning over many lifetimes, where you relive different relationships and learn karmic lessons. This is a subject that I recommend you study and give a lot of thought to as you get older. Knowledge, time and life experiences will help you decide where you stand on this vital issue.

Suicide, depression and sadness

We spoke extensively in chapter 5 about negative emotions. Sadness and depression are more normal parts of the human experience than they are negative. They only form a problem if they take over your mind and behaviour to an abnormal degree. Who decides what is 'abnormal'? You can yourself. If you're waking up every morning feeling down, if you feel stressed-out all the time, if you lack enthusiasm and energy for even the most basic tasks, you are moving into a state of chronic depression. Everyone feels 'blue' at times and that's fine; if you just let it be, it'll pass naturally. If you have a persistent problem that you can't seem to solve, that could get you down for a while, but, again, as things improve, you feel better.

As a teenager, you're liable to feel 'depressed' a fair bit of the time. Your parents probably complain that you're moody and withdrawn. You just want to be left alone to sulk in your room when you're in that grumpy space. You would think that stress and depression have very little in common as stress is about heightened awareness and depression is feeling pressed down, flat. Yet, there is a distinct link between these two states. Too much stress can cause depression as the psyche strives for its natural balance. That's why, after a period of change or excitement, you can easily go into a slump emotionally. A sense of anti-climax takes over; it's common after holidays or a terrific party or an exam period. All these feelings are normal and, if you expect them, they don't have to bug you so much.

Here are some strategies for managing depression:

Depression notes

Factors controlling Depression
- Stress
- Coping strategies
- Self-image
- Focus of the anxiety
- Self-generating worry
- Insecurity/self doubt

Symptoms
- Irritability
- Insomnia
- Inability to relax
- Inability to concentrate
- Crying

- Dependence
- Withdrawal
- Inertia/Lethargy

Strategies to handle Depression
- Action
- Breathing space/distancing/centring
- Willingness to change
- Faith and positive thinking
- Physical health
- Attitude
- Share your problem
- Letting go
- Make a list of things that make you happy
- Make a list of things that make you unhappy
- Diminish the negative; emphasise the positive. What do you want from life?
- Unhappiness, though undesirable, is still comfortable, so take a chance on change

For any number of reasons, some people can't bounce emotions off as well as others. If you are a teenager who tends to take life seriously, who takes things to heart, as they say, you may take longer to heal than one who rolls with the punches and accepts life as it comes. I can't say anything to make your situation easier for you, as only living and experiencing will teach you what is worth crying over and what isn't. What concerns me is the fact of your age. Being a teenager makes you much more vulnerable to the ups and downs of daily life. A small rejection can seem to be a major disaster, a pimple before a date a catastrophe, and a failing grade the end of the world.

If these stressful events happen often enough in a week or month, the pressure starts to mount and death, rather than a distant event, can begin to look desirable as an escape. Alcohol and drugs are temporary escapes from the pain and conflicts of life, but you can always stop using those. Death as a solution is permanent. Suicide is the ultimate betrayal of yourself and life. It is rushing to a premature death instead of staying to find out how much better things can be.

Some of you reading this book may have thought about ending your life when things got tough; some of you may be thinking about suicide as a real alternative right now. Yes, it is an alternative you can choose, but why not choose life instead? It's too painful, you reply. Life *is* painful, but it's also beautiful and wonderful, the best and most special of all gifts. If a loved friend brought you an imperfect gift, would you not still treasure it because of the giver? That's how it is with life. Even at its most difficult points, it is a gift from our parents, the creator and the universe. How can we take it for granted or throw it away?

Thousands of teenagers do every day all over the world, so let's look realistically at why it happens. Suicide is the ultimate aloneness. It screams out the message that the person feels totally and utterly isolated from every other human being. That's why the world readily believed that Marilyn Monroe committed suicide; we were told she spent many hours prior to her death phoning friends, reaching out for the love and attention she craved, only to be rejected time and again. New evidence has come out that she might have been murdered, but at the time, we all felt the pathos of that beautiful yet lonely woman, alone, desperate, calling out in the night for comfort. Perhaps many of you have felt like that. I know I have, and the pain seems unendurable. But if you can just get through the night, there is always a bright new morning. Now, if I ever feel really sad or lonely, I just ask my spiritual guides to walk with me through the darkness and help me into the light. It never fails. Try it. Of course, you have to ask with all your heart and really believe it.

When you wake up, you may still have the same problems you went to sleep with, but you will also have the inner peace you forged with your pain and your faith. Then, you can start again. This all comes back to valuing yourself. What problem in life can be more important than precious, wonderful you?

Do you think there's anything your parents could be so angry about that they wouldn't care more for you?

The futility of suicide became very clear to me when I was in hospital once. A fellow patient, a young woman, had tried to commit suicide, unsuccessfully — it was her third attempt. Her body had suffered toxic shock from all the sleeping tablets she had swallowed and the girl was unable to walk or even move for several days. When she was finally conscious and able to speak, I asked her about her experiences. (This was before I became a counsellor, but I've always been interested in people, and especially in why they do things.) She told me that each time she had attempted suicide, something always stopped it working. The message of this was so clear to me, I wondered how it could have escaped the girl's notice. So I asked, 'Don't you think you're not meant to die, that there's something you're meant to hang around for?' She said she hadn't thought of that.

With love, nothing is insurmountable. Never forget that. Love has many faces. Reach out to those around you. If you're feeling sad, tell someone. Phone a helpline. See a counsellor. Choose life, never death.

Crossroads, decisions, change

Life is one long series of crossroads where you have to make a choice or decision before moving on. Often, the path ahead is not clear at the time and that's why decision-making is a particularly difficult skill for many people. Making a good decision requires three steps: weighing up all the factors involved; letting your intuition guide you; and accepting the consequences of the decision.

Where there is a lot at stake, indecision or what we call procrastination is often practised, and that makes the decision-making process so much more difficult to conquer. What happens is that negative thinking is allowed to take over — fear, doubt and anxiety, in particular, block your ability to act. You are at an age where you're just starting to have to make decisions for yourself: what car to buy, what course to study, whether or not to leave home, how to spend your money, and so on. Being a teenager is all about change. You stand at the very crossroads of adult life and, as much as you long to choose your way and get going, there's also a lot of fear associated with change, especially as, in life, we can rarely turn back. Caution is wise, but not so much that you fall into inaction. Risk-taking is also part and parcel of human existence.

The middle road is the safest, of course, but sometimes, life gives you little choice but to plunge into a radical decision or action. Once you've really thought about it, take a chance and go for it.

Dreams and nightmares

One important component in your spiritual armour lies in the realm of the dream world that each of us inhabits at night. You may or may not remember your dreams in the morning but, in this section, I want to outline for you the importance of dreams, how they reflect your subconscious state and how you can learn to recall them.

This is a complex psychological area, and I don't propose to bog you down in all the various theories. Let me just say that the research being done at present is uncovering some incredible data about our dream lives, such as dreamers arranging to meet at appointed times during the night in a designated place, and actually carrying this out! You've all no doubt seen the *Nightmare on Elm Street* series of films. While they are fiction and designed to frighten moviegoers, there's actually quite a lot of accurate material in them about dreaming and dreamers.

For most of you, dreams are either not recalled at all or just a series of hazy images. It takes desire and practice to consistently remember your dreams in detail. I've been practising for several years, and can now recall in precise detail anything up to five or six dreams every night. But what's the point, you might ask. To answer this, you need at least a basic understanding of what dreams are. They are the symbolic expression of your subconscious fears, anxieties, feelings, hopes, and so on. Some are simply a reworking of these from the day's events; for example, you see a movie with Michael Douglas in it and you dream of him that night.

These sorts of experiences are not meaningful in the psychological sense. But dreams can also express the many unresolved emotions and conditions of the day, and that's where they can help us live our lives more positively. For example, you're having problems with a certain teacher at school and you're holding onto a tidal wave of emotion you can't get out, perhaps not even fully aware of how angry and resentful you really are. One night, after you've had some dealings with that teacher during the day, you dream of killing him/her. This doesn't mean that you really want to kill or physically hurt; it's a symbolic expression of how you feel — that you want to 'get rid' of that person. If you understand this, it's a great way to release some of the hostility instead of having an actual confrontation.

Sometimes, by dreaming through a desire or a great emotional distress, you can actually resolve it. I've seen this happen many times in counselling. For instance, a man who had severe emotional problems relived, through counselling, being beaten by his stepfather as a teenager, and being very cruelly put down and abused. I suggested to him that he go to his stepfather and confront him with the pain he'd caused. The man said he couldn't imagine doing that, mainly because he didn't want to hurt his mother, who was unaware of the problem. One night, he dreamt that he was with his stepfather in the counselling room and he proceeded to tell him exactly what he felt. He woke up crying, as though a great floodgate had been released, and he felt at peace for the first time in years.

Dreams also reflect moods experienced during the day.

For example, you will tend to have anxiety dreams if you're worried about something in your life, and you might dream of beautiful scenes, sunshine and laughing if you're relaxed and happy. Much dream symbolism can be readily understood in the light of day, such as feeling overwhelmed by waves or being chased or falling.

Nightmares

What are nightmares, and why do you get them? Very few of us can say that we have never experienced a nightmare. You know how scary they are, how you wake up cold and terrified, sometimes screaming or sobbing. When you were a child, a parent soothed those demons away and they were rarely a problem unless you had scary dreams often. Now, you may remember what it was that frightened you. In place of that nameless 'monster' is possibly something identifiable. For a girl, it might be being stalked by a dark figure at night; for a boy, it might be being thrown off a motorbike at horrible speeds. These scary experiences and the terrors they evoke are usually related to real fears you have about your daily life. It's very important for your subconscious mind to get them out, and dreams are a safe and effective way for this to happen.

As a general rule, nightmares are normal and not anything to worry about, but if you have one that recurs, you need to look into it and seek professional help if it doesn't stop.

Recurring dreams

Why do dreams recur? Some dreams occur to give your conscious mind a message. While most dream adventures are cryptic and take time and practice to decipher, some are as clear as a bell. The message may come in the form of a person you know saying something to you or a specific event that has a distinct meaning. Sometimes, a person who is dead or from your past will appear in dreams to make contact. A few nights after my mother died, I saw her in a beautiful golden carriage. She stepped down and was dressed in a glittering gown, young and beautiful again. She spoke to me very gently, telling me not to worry about her as she was fine. You can imagine that dream gave me a lot of peace and relief at the time.

If you take no notice of the dream message, however, you might start to have a recurring dream. It becomes like a persistent tap on your shoulder. If you ignore it, it won't go away but rather gets more insistent, until you finally have to look around and find out what the message is. That's what happens with a recurring dream. Whatever it deals with in your life is not being resolved, so it keeps coming. You may need some help from a reputable book about dream analysis or an expert therapist to work through this. Eventually, as you change the situation in your waking life, you will no longer need to have the dream. This is particularly important with recurring nightmares, which can become very draining as they disturb sleep and some people actually feel too scared to fall asleep in case they have 'that horrible dream' again.

While nightmares are happening, there are ways to ease the fears and anxieties. Experts suggest that a 'dream weapon' should be taken into sleep. This doesn't have to be a real weapon, like a knife or club, but rather a symbolic object that makes the dreamer feel safe. If this is applicable to you, you might feel that it's a bit 'babyish' to have a protective teddy or doll, especially if you're a guy, but believe me, age doesn't come into it. It does work, and it's better to try something simple and positive than suffer nightmares or have to take drugs in order to sleep.

The dream weapon acts as a soother for both your conscious and subconscious mind, and remember what we said earlier in the chapter about the power of the mind. You can 'control' almost anything that happens to you by thinking the right thoughts. There are documented cases of cancer sufferers curing themselves of their disease by the strength of their healthy thoughts, by using meditation, positive affirmations and creative visualisation to conquer their fears and, thus, their illness.

Even if you are a natural dream recaller, you still lose a lot of your dream memories when you wake. Those of you who don't think you dream at all, think again! It is a scientifically proven fact that every human being dreams every night, and here's another amazing fact: after decades of research into sleep deprivation, experts have now proved that it is *dream* deprivation that causes emotional and psychological breakdown. So don't underestimate the importance of those weird experiences and visions you have at night. They keep us sane!

Recaller or non-recaller, you can practise remembering your dreams. Here are some simple and basic tips for recalling your dreams:

- First, buy a dream journal. It doesn't have to be anything fancy, just a normal exercise pad, but it must be kept only for dream recording and left by the side of your bed at all times. It should be right next to your sleeping head so that you don't have to fumble for it if you wake during the night with a vivid dream. With it should be an easily accessible pen, and both should be kept near a nightlight.
- Before you go to sleep each night, say a prayer to your dream guide and ask him or her to walk with you during your dream journeys. Write the day's date on a clean page as that signals to your subconscious that you expect to remember your dreams. Dr Joyce Brothers, the American psychologist, suggests that if you have a particular problem you're seeking an answer to, you can ask your subconscious mind to work on it during the night. Your first thought the next morning should provide an insight into a solution.
- When you first begin, you may have to wake up several times during the night to write your dreams down while they're fresh. After a few nights of this, you may wish you'd never started! However, it doesn't continue once you've trained your subconscious mind to hold the memories till morning. Sometimes now, after years of deliberate dream

recall, I can wake up with details of five or six dreams quite clear in my mind. At other times, I wake with a sense of just having had an interesting dream but I can't remember it, so I just ask my dream guide for help and all the details flood my mind as I lie in that semi-conscious state between sleep and awakening.

Obviously, you can't expect spectacular results when you first start, but it's a worthwhile pursuit — and what could be more fascinating than the workings of your own subconscious mind?

Social life and leisure

This should be an area of total joy in life, but not for you teenagers! You put so much stock on acceptance, appearance and 'scoring'! There is so much more emphasis on success than effort. That's why I wanted to make a brief mention of the whole concept of 'leisure' in this section. Leisure is essentially time that belongs to you exclusively.

For teenagers, this is associated with having a good time, raging, making out, hanging around or lolling about! Creative leisure comes much later in life. Yet, it's good to practise using time well. As we saw earlier in the book, time management is a key stress management technique. In terms of personal and spiritual growth, the main question is: are you spending your time positively or negatively? If you're hanging around just killing time, or getting up to mischief, or bored out of your minds, I think you know the answer.

Being happy is not the same as having a good time because happiness doesn't end when the good time is over. Happiness is a state of mind, and it can exist even in the darkest place and under the most unpleasant conditions. You can cultivate it and nurture it, but don't forget that it's never a permanent state. You can have the happiest day, and then something awful happens and your mood changes. That's just the changeability of life. Nothing lasts, so when you're in a bad space, you can console yourself with that thought. When you're feeling terrific, it's a fool's paradise to expect to stay like that forever. The happiest people are those who have learnt this secret and adapt to change in a spirit of acceptance and adventure. I'm still working on that one myself!

Keep in mind the two words, moderation and balance. Cater to all your different needs, physical, emotional, spiritual and mental. Feed your curiosity now so that it becomes a lifetime habit. You can just as easily die from boredom as you can from disease, as we see when old people simply lose the will to live and fade away. You will always stay young, no matter how many years you live, if you stay interested in a variety of things, keep active and healthy, and love life.

To sum up this chapter and this book, let me just say that life can be a joy or a struggle — it's up to you. You were given a certain start by your parents, positive or negative as the case may be, but what happens from now on is entirely up to you. You can choose to live your life blaming chance or luck or God when things go wrong and taking all the credit when things are right, or you can accept that you are responsible for your own happiness at all times.

Another choice you have is whether you wish to see yourself as special and wonderful, which each of us is, or concentrate on all the things you don't like about yourself and all the things you don't have. Positive or negative. A daily choice.

The human spirit is absolutely indomitable. Many thousands of people through history have done things that they were told were 'impossible'. Men and women have lived through wars and other unspeakable horrors, conquered mountains, learnt to fly, discovered cures for diseases, given of themselves in countless ways. Don't let the doom-mongers tell you that life is pointless and that everyone's only out for themselves. The evidence is all around you that it's simply not true. We may not be able to examine love under a microscope but we can see its effects every day, everywhere. Love of self, of family and of country are still noble pursuits.

Do some little thing every day that is just to make the world better. Instead of littering, go to a deserted beach and pick up any rubbish you see lying around; feed some birds in the park; help out a friend who's short of money. But don't do it for the look of appreciation in her/his eyes or the praise or even the satisfaction. Just do it, and watch your joys multiply. Don't take my word for it. Go out and try it.

My final advice is: be true to yourself, be brave but, most of all, be happy.

Only as high as I reach can I grow.
Only as far as I seek can I go.
Only as deep as I look can I see.
Only as much as I dream can I be.
                                        KAREN RIVEN

9 The A to Z of Stress

As I said in the foreword to this book, I cannot hope to cover all the big and little things that are potentially stressful for you. Every single day, even now, someone will make another suggestion to me for inclusion and I have to say, 'Stop, I have to draw the line somewhere!' No doubt, even when the book is finished and on the shelves, I will still be thinking of important points I missed out.

This glossary is an attempt to reduce that likelihood as much as possible. It lists many topics I would have liked to say more about but just couldn't; also, some of the less general issues which only affect a small percentage of you.

Use this chapter as a reference. A stress you may not have in your life right now could crop up next week or next month. Here goes.

Abortion/adoption

Both highly emotive and personal issues. I can't tell you what the right moral decision is but if you find yourself pregnant or your girlfriend is, take a great deal of care and find out all the facts before you decide on abortion, adoption or keeping the baby. Whichever decision you make, it's going to affect all three of you and your families for the rest of your lives. Confide in your parents if you can, and seek professional, unbiased advice. Get counselling after any one of the three courses of action, as accepting the consequences is very difficult after such an emotional episode.

Abuse

This can take many forms, but is usually grouped under the headings: physical abuse, psychological abuse and emotional abuse. If you are a victim of *any* kind of abuse, seek medical and/or legal help. Prolonged abuse will take its toll on you and affect many areas of your life.

Accident

One of the most stressful events that can happen to you. Statistically, teenagers have more accidents than other age-groups, and these are often linked to alcohol. Don't drink and drive, and *never* forget that the car is a lethal weapon. Never fool around behind the wheel — and put your seatbelts on! An accident is a shock to the nervous system so don't try to tough it out. Rest and take it easy for a few days. Obviously, get injuries checked out.

Aches and pains

Backache, headaches, etc. are both a cause and a symptom of stress. They are usually linked to emotional problems if not caused by illness. Tension is the culprit, so stress reduction is the best cure. Backache can be helped by improving posture, sitting properly, and exercise.

Aggression

Very stressful if you're at the wrong end of it. If you're dishing it out, you're probably under too much stress! Stay out of places where people get drunk and throw their weight around, especially if you're female. Walk away if you can. Never try to reason with someone who's drunk or power-crazy. If you're being aggressive, look at your lifestyle, health and diet. Speak very softly to an aggressive person and try to diffuse the situation. If it's someone you know, try to get to the heart of the problem with them once the tension has relaxed. Your own aggression is hard to manage on the spot. If you feel it rising up, deep breathing and counting to ten does work.

AIDS

Prevention of AIDS has been discussed in the book but the stress of this disease cannot be overlooked. You're unlikely to have the condition at your age, and if you restrict sexual activity and use condoms, you should stay safe. If you're unlucky enough to know someone with AIDS, remember you can't catch the virus with casual contact so don't feel tempted to stay away or withdraw the gift of your friendship. Get as much information as you can from the experts.

Alienation/isolation

The stress of these comes from feeling cut off from other people. We can all feel like this at times but an extreme inability to connect and communicate can cause severe depression and lead to mental illness or suicide. Sociologists often speak of the alienation of cities because they don't foster close ties or neighbourly contact. As individuals, we can reduce isolation by reaching out to others even if we feel shy or inept ourselves. Forming friendships, staying close to our families, helping people where we can — these will go a long way to ensuring that we stay in touch with ourselves and those around us.

Allergies

Australians suffer from a wide range of these, and they are the cause and consequence of a lot of stress. Check out foods and other common allergy-causing items that may bring on your symptoms. Keep your home as clean and dust-free as possible. Allergies are believed to relate to anxiety as well as physical causes, so try to reduce stress in your life. As with so many other things, stress can be a cause and a result. Seek medical help if your condition is chronic.

Animals

They don't cause stress, but rather can be used as a stress reducer. It has been scientifically proven that patting and stroking an animal reduces stress in humans. Looking after them may cause some stress but, on the whole, animals are delightful soothers. Remember that we share the earth with all living things, and they deserve your respect and compassion always.

Avoidance/denial

Can cause a lot of stress if it's a prolonged condition. Refusal to talk about and deal with problems in our lives suppresses our feelings and brings on tension and anxiety.

Breaking up

Most people would list this as one of the most stressful experiences you can have. There's no way to avoid this happening in your life totally. You just have to remind yourself that time heals, and try not to repeat the same mistakes. If one person wants to break up and the other doesn't it's far more painful, but even when it's a mutual decision, some pain and lots of stress can be expected.

Cancer

I've singled out this disease over others because it is a major killer in our society and is linked specifically to the incidence of stress. Whether you or one of your loved ones gets cancer, it will undoubtedly be one of the greatest challenges of your life. But cancer is not the death sentence it used to be and early detection is the important factor. Prevention is strongly recommended. Cancer hits all ages, but as a teenager, you can set up lifestyle habits that will help you avoid some of the most common cancers; for example, bowel cancer is less likely to develop where there is a balanced, high-fibre diet; lung cancer is largely caused by a combination of stress and smoking; for females, regular self-examination will detect early breast cancer; for all teenagers, the important warning about not overdoing that great Australian pastime, sunbaking. As with so many things, moderation is the answer. Melanoma is a great Australian killer; don't be a tanned corpse.

Cities

City life is understandably more stressful than life in the country. With noise, pollution, crime, traffic and other hazards to contend with, city dwellers are bombarded on a daily basis with stressful events. On the other hand, cities offer many benefits and diversions. Choose where you want to live as an adult according to your temperament.

Compulsive/obsessive behaviour

Feeling the need to behave compulsively is extremely stressful as it brings on anxiety and depletes energy. Comparatively few people suffer the extreme forms, but almost every one of us is compulsive in some way, such as with tidiness, insisting things are done by our methods, overdoing things such as making lists or giving instructions. Almost any area of life can become compulsive if we let it. Once locked in, it's difficult to break out of its grip and that in itself is stressful. Compulsions also cause a great deal of stress in relationships.

Crime

Very stressful. You may not be directly affected but you can't avoid being aware of it all around you, particularly in cities. Your movements may be limited, especially if you're female; for example, not being able to go into certain places and areas at night. Crime as a social problem is an ongoing challenge for law-makers and police. Specific crimes such as murder and rape bring indescribable stress if they touch your life, but awareness of crime in general is also stressful, and involves having to secure your home against burglary, lock up your car, keep your money in a safe place, etc.

Crisis

Crisis is usually understood to be either an unexpected stress event, such as a home fire, or an ongoing problem that has become radical because of its prolonged nature. An example of the latter might be a family situation. There are crisis agencies listed in the phone book for a sudden onset; if you're locked into circumstances that have become chronic, seek professional help. A general tip is to remain calm in any sort of crisis as panic will make things worse.

Crowds

Being pushed along or squashed into a crowd isn't much fun and often brings on bad temper, which is a sure sign that you're under stress! If you know they bother you, avoid places and times when you're likely to be caught up in a crowd. Claustrophobia (fear of tight spaces) can result if you're in a crowd and feel you can't get out.

Disasters

Obviously, natural and man-made disasters bring in their wake tremendous stress. There is no easy way to recover from the effects. My best advice is to get counselling if you're ever involved in a fire, earthquake, shoot-out, robbery, explosion or similar event. There are professionals who specialise in dealing with the aftershock of frightening, life-changing happenings.

Discrimination

This is a general term for the stress of being judged on the basis of your age, sex, race, etc. Being a teenager probably feels like one long discrimination at times, but remember some of the restrictions you have to endure now are necessary so that you make fewer mistakes than you might. Of course, if you are unfairly treated because of being your age, a girl or an Aboriginal, that's a different matter, and disallowed by law. Check out your rights in this area.

Divorce

This is unlikely to happen to you at your age, but if it happens within your family, it causes long-lasting stress. I have counselled adults who still talk of the hurt they felt when their parents split up years ago. Divorce rocks the foundations of a family's security and its painful effects should not be underestimated. Sometimes, family counselling is the only way for the wounds to be healed. If this is happening in your home, don't hesitate to call for help, as being brave will only internalise the pain and cause problems for you in future years. Also, consider the difficult time your parents are going through and try not to lay blame or add to their troubles.

Gay parents

If you live with two men or two women as your 'parents', you may find it difficult to reconcile this with the families of your friends and peers. The idea of every family consisting of Mum, Dad and kids may still be the ideal but is becoming less and less common. Family are those who love and care for you, and the combination of gender shouldn't matter. You may not like it now but hopefully, in future years, you'll come to appreciate that love is what matters. The other possibility is that one of your parents decides he/she wants to lead a gay lifestyle, and leave the family unit. This parent will need all your love and compassion even if you feel terribly betrayed. At first it will cause grave hurt and extreme stress, but your relationships with this parent can be restored so let time heal and try not to judge too harshly.

Harassment

I once counselled a teenage girl who worked in a deli. Her boss made sexual advances to her every chance he got, finding excuses to keep her working late. When she tried to dissuade him, she was threatened with dismissal. This is not an uncommon story and happens to both boys and girls. If you find yourself a victim of sexual harassment, remember that it's a legal offence. It's the secrecy that causes the stress because you give the perpetrator power over you. The harassment will continue until you say no and report him/her.

Homelessness

This is obviously a major stress for those of you who are living through it. There are many government and church agencies that offer accommodation and counselling, but ultimately this is a social problem and relates to family life. The only reason for you to be homeless is because you can't make it at home. The problem could lie in your parents' attitude or yours; resolving this is even more important than where you live. Homelessness is the ultimate rebellion on your part and the ultimate rejection from your parents. It's easy to walk out of home when you're angry or the stress is simply too great, but it's very difficult to walk back in. Your pride won't let you, and both sides are waiting for the other to give in. If you have the choice of staying on the streets or making it up and returning home, think about it very carefully as homelessness can become a way of life. There are also many inherent dangers and temptations to face, and an uncertain future.

Illness

In chapter 6, I wrote of the link between stress and illness, and in chapter 8 about the effects of mind power on health. If you find yourself ill, this is a different form of stress. Depression and irritability are often symptoms of such common conditions as 'flu and stomach infections. When you're a teenager, the last thing you want is to languish in bed when your friends are out having fun. If you haven't got a parent who's at home, you can also get bored and lonely. The secret is to stay well by living with minimum stress in your life, and keep to natural remedies, such as vitamin therapy, fresh air and exercise, as far as possible. If you do go down with a 'bug', grin and bear it, get lots of rest, and try to use the time as profitably as you can.

Incest

This was the subject I chose to leave out of chapters 1 and 4, where it might have belonged, because this was to be a general book about teenage stress, and incest is a very specific human problem. I don't think I have to tell you it's extremely stressful. It's also a very complex issue and affects the victim, the perpetrator and everyone else in the family. Incest may not happen in the immediate family circle, but regardless of this, touches everyone near. A lot of the stress of incest is caused by the secrecy that surrounds it. There's also shame, a loss of innocence and a betrayal of trust. The effects of incest continue for many years, long after the incest itself is over. Expert counselling is absolutely essential so that the pain can be released and forgiveness for self and perpetrator can happen.

Intelligence

Intelligence shouldn't be a cause of stress but it can be, in two ways. If you're exceptionally bright, you may feel under a lot of pressure to perform. Well-meaning parents can make you feel that you have to live up to a certain standard at all times. A very clever friend of mine got six distinctions for his school-leaving subjects and was asked by his family why he hadn't got seven! Work hard, but never forget the importance of fun and relaxation. If you're not academically clever or just an average student, there may be stress from ridicule or being told that you're lazy and not performing 'to capacity'. Apart from doing your best and resisting the pressure, relax in the thought that you will find your niche later in life.

Kissing

This is stressful if you're not sure whether you should or shouldn't, or even how! At your age, kissing is a very natural part of sexual experimentation; just keep in mind that it is a form of foreplay so you need to be aware that it can lead to heavier things. If you don't feel ready or you're scared of what it might lead to, keep the kissing light and brief, rather than get into French kissing, which is prolonged and uses the tongue. Another form of stress is avoiding a kiss without giving offence. This was covered in chapter 4. As far as worrying about whether you can kiss well or not, it's a perfectly natural activity and improves with practice. There's no need to be anxious about it.

Law/police

Only stressful if you're at the wrong end! You can get into trouble by being stupid and breaking the law, or it can be quite inadvertent. In either case, you need sound legal advice. The police can be either your friend or your enemy depending on your attitude to them. You should attempt to acquaint yourself with basic civil laws and also your rights, whether or not you have ever been caught for anything.

Lies

Lies are very stressful to those who tell them and those who receive them. I am now almost obsessively honest, yet for a short time, when I was about 8, 9 years old, I used to lie compulsively. I think it's a stage most children go through but, as a teenager, you may also find yourself in that lying pattern. Why do people lie? Most commonly, to avoid trouble or out of fear and/or embarrassment. If you feel cornered and blurt a lie out, it may be difficult to undo it, but, if you have a chance to stop and think, consider that you are probably compounding the original problem by adding a lie to it. Honesty is often not the softest option in life but, in the long run, it's usually the simplest and best.

Living conditions

These can be very stressful if they don't suit your temperament. It's not just the quality and trappings of a home, but the atmosphere and the things that go on around you. Some of you may live in mansions but would prefer a more modest home; others may have to share a room, so privacy and quiet are what you long for. An unhappy environment is one of the most stressful conditions to live with, so do what you can to lessen the tension. As far as the style of home you come from is concerned — dirty, busy, untidy, joyful, noisy, quiet — that's the luck of the draw. If you don't like it, you can create a different type for yourself in the future.

Loneliness

Loneliness is different from solitude or aloneness, which can be desirable and anything but stressful. It's stressful to be alone when you don't wish to be. Everyone feels this way sometimes but teenagers probably more than most. The best way to combat it is to learn to enjoy your leisure so that you don't feel the need to fill every minute. I grew up as an only child and learnt early to amuse myself. As a result, I rarely get bored and relish time apart and quiet. If you belong to a large family, it's a lot more difficult to have this capacity but you can train yourself into it. Of course, sometimes, you will feel miserable and self-pitying, wanting to be alone yet hating it. That's called being human. There's nothing to do but get through it.

Loss

Any loss is stressful, whether it's a pen on the morning of an exam or a friend, a pet or a loved one in death. No life is possible without loss, and I can't say anything that will reduce the pain. Once again, your attitude will make the biggest difference. You can see loss as a beginning or an ending. Either way, time is the only cure.

Marriage

Some of you will marry as teenagers, taking on all the challenges of this institution as well as the handicap of your age. I personally think teenage marriages have little chance of success, and the statistics bear me out. But there are teenage marriages that work very well, due either to the mature attitudes of the couple or to other factors being in their favour, such as having employment and a place to live, waiting to have a family and so on. I married at twenty and feel even that was too young — as my subsequent divorce would seem to prove. The main problem is that you don't know enough about yourself and what you want to make a lifelong commitment to another person. If you can wait, do so.

Money

Money is usually only stressful if we have too little of it or if we've spent more than we have. This results in debt, which is very stressful indeed if allowed to get out of hand. Money itself is intrinsically neither good or bad. It is a commodity to be used. Budgeting and attitudes to money are covered in chapter 7, but it is important to emphasise in this section that money causes more stress and conflict than almost any other single item in the human repertoire of problems. And, yet, money need not be a problem. Like stress, it needs to be managed. At your age, credit cards are a huge temptation but, remember, you still pay when you use credit; the only differences are the delay factor and added costs. There are ways and means to get what you want, such as saving towards a target or using a lay-by system. Don't fall for the instant gratification trap. Sometimes, it's even more fun when you have to wait. The habits you set up now regarding money will make the difference between a comfortable lifestyle, even if you're on low wages, or a life of forever balancing the books and coming out uneven. Money is with you throughout your life, so you may as well make a friend of it.

Mothers

The most wonderful of people as perpetuated in popular fiction, but in reality just human beings who try to do their best. The role of mother does not automatically make a woman clever or wise or caring. There are just as many selfish, cruel, mean, cold, foolish mothers around as there are good ones. The only thing that distinguishes this relationship is that it is unique in the human experience. So is the father role, of course, but that's not as influential on us as the mother one, especially in the case of daughters. Who we are and grow up to become are largely the result of who our mothers are. This puts a huge burden of responsibility on mothers, and society loves to heap guilt on 'inadequate' mothers who beat their children or give them away or neglect them. A far more beneficial exercise would be to remember that they are just people with their own needs and to learn from them all we can, good or bad. In that way, we grow to our own potential and can look back without guilt or reproach. If you are a teenage mother, be gentle with yourself as you have a harder road to tread than older mothers. Ask for advice and help; don't try to do it alone. If you're lucky, you will have your boyfriend or family and friends to stand by you, but many of you will not. Single mums, you are everywhere in today's society. It's a tough way to go, but either by choice or by necessity, you're out there struggling to make ends meet and care for your children. Many of you will have full or part-time jobs as well, and you lack the support of a loving partner. Stress is probably your constant companion, but don't let it take over your life. Check out all your options, look after your health and include other people in your life, especially positive male friends who can be a healthy role model for your child.

Moving house

One of the most high-ranking stress experiences. It's stressful for a number of reasons. Firstly, it involves a major change. Next, it requires a great deal of organising, time and effort. The act of moving is stress-ridden in itself, and when it's over, the work's just beginning! The only way to minimise the stress of moving is to have a positive attitude about where you're going to and to be well-prepared *before* the event. Maintaining a cheerful mood will also work wonders and positively affect those around you.

Noise

All forms of noise are stressful, not only in the emotional but also in the physical sense. It's difficult to have a tranquil mind in the middle of loud music or traffic or children screaming. We saw in chapter 2 the importance of a peaceful environment for homework and study. That's no less true for other activities in which you are involved. Of course, teenagers love loud music and that's okay as long as you're not trying to do mental work at the same time and you protect your ears from prolonged exposure! Minimise the effects of living in a noisy century by balancing the input with some quieter sounds. Some people fear the silence and fill up the quiet with as much noise as possible. If this applies to you learn to offset this.

Politics

A sensitive subject to a lot of people. Again, families tend to expect you to continue in their voting tradition. Voting is a privilege, although many see it as a nuisance. As you get older, find out at least the basics about each party so that your vote counts for something. If you choose to support Labor when your family has always voted Liberal or vice-versa, there's likely to be conflict, especially if your family feels very strongly about politics. Stick to your guns and talk about it as little as possible!

Premenstrual syndrome

For teenagers, this is only applicable to girls. Later in life, males will also be affected by the stress of PMS. It's the tension felt by females just prior to their periods. It varies in intensity from girl to girl but when it's severe, it can be unbearable. This, combined with the pain of menstruation, can keep some girls in bed for a couple of days. At best, it makes you irritable and hard to live with. Vitamin B6 is said to help, and just knowing about it means you can learn to live with it for those few days every month.

Privacy

You are apt to be very big on privacy, as teenagers are rather secretive creatures. You either keep a personal diary or you hate the idea of your mother looking through your drawers while you're out. As a stress factor, though, privacy takes on a wider meaning. Invasion of personal space is something you would relate to. That's when someone gets closer to you than you want them to or talks to you while you're reading or thinking. You probably keep to yourself a lot at home and expect your privacy to be respected. If it isn't, it can cause a good deal of family stress. Home represents a haven to many people, not just in a physical sense but in a psychological way, as well. That's why victims of burglaries speak of being 'violated' or 'invaded'. In a society, there are very definite boundaries between people, ranging from tangible ones like fences around a house to unseen ones like social rules for behaviour. Like it or not, they are necessary to preserve order and maintain privacy, thus reducing the potential for conflict between people, especially those living in close proximity such as family members and neighbours in a suburban street.

Racism

If you're at the wrong end of it because of your nationality and/or colour, I don't have to tell you how stressful and humiliating it is. Most racism is borne of ignorance and fear. Kids are taught to feel this way by their parents, and it's passed on without thought. Be proud of your race and try to forgive those who tease you or are cruel. If you've been taught that some races are inferior, determine to be the one to break this belief pattern. The buck can stop with you, and you'll be contributing to a better world. All people are worthy and special and blessed. Don't let anyone tell you otherwise.

Rape

This is one of the ultimate disempowerments. It is now widely accepted that rape is an act of violence rather than sex, but because it violates your most private being, it takes away a lot more than your choice. It robs you of dignity, self-esteem and trust, and it can happen to you whether you're male or female. Most rapes occur through someone known to the victim but, of course, there are also random cases that occur late at night in the streets or as a result of a house break-in. No matter what the circumstances, you must *never* feel responsible. You are always innocent. It takes a lot of time and courage to get over rape, so get counselling for as long as you feel you need it. The important thing is not to allow this one act to rob you of all your future joy. This can happen if you keep reliving the experience in your mind and/or constantly imagine it recurring. Eventually, you have to let go and forgive, and with professional help, you can.

Rejection

This is very stressful and hard to take at any age. Again, it is linked to self-esteem. If you feel good about yourself, you're less likely to be devastated by someone saying no to you, whether on a personal or business matter. Feel the disappointment, feel the pain but then bounce back, knowing that we all get rejected at different times and the ones who succeed are those who never give up in their hearts. Teenage life is all about rejection and there's no shame whatsoever in it, only in giving up.

Roles

Each of you play multiple roles in your daily lives. You are daughters/sons, nephews/nieces, friends, citizens, neighbours, grandchildren, cousins, students; the list is endless. These are designated roles and you may resent them at your age. The trick is to play them in your external life while keeping the integrity of your own individuality. That's always going to be one of the biggest challenges of living in a society. Sometimes, too, your roles will clash, and you'll have difficult decisions to make. Think of it as acting a part in a stage play — just don't ever lose sight of who you really are.

Sexual frustration

As a teenager, you are likely to experience sexual frustration constantly as you lack the suitable outlets for your feelings and physical needs. At puberty, you have sensations and tensions that you can't identify. Then, as you progress through the teenage years, you start dating and being sexually attracted to others; your emotions become more focused but, of course, they can be misleading as you are relating with your hormones and not your mind or heart. Instead of easing the frustration, you may now actually feel more because you want to have sex but can't. If you're a boy, this situation is probably on your mind a lot of the time. You're thinking either about sex in general or about how to have it, how to have more, the many ways to do it, which girls to do it with, etc. That's perfectly natural, but keep in mind that sex is not only a biological activity. It has emotional and psychological consequences, so before you consider making out, do some checking out. That goes for boys and girls. This is too serious a matter to act impulsively over. Care for each other and yourselves and you won't go wrong. As for the stress of sexual frustration, remember sexual tension is pent-up energy which can easily be diverted. So, keep active and focus your mind onto other matters until such time as sex is the right thing to do.

Television

It's very easy to become addicted to TV as it's essentially a passive form of entertainment. It's easy and relaxed — in fact, a good aid to stress management. Where it becomes a problem, as with so many other things, is if it's overdone. It can cause alienation and conflict within family life — people use it as an excuse not to communicate. It can keep you from exercising, going out, socialising, making an effort. The key word is control. You *are* in control, you can choose when and what you want to watch, especially with VCRs allowing you to record shows that you can watch later. Television is a fantastic form of entertainment and education. Use it for those reasons and not to avoid life.

Traffic

Stressful not only because of the noise but because the mental concentration required to negotiate your way through it causes a lot of pressure. Then, there's the frustration and the time-wasting aspects. If you live in one of the larger cities, even if you're not a driver yourself, you no doubt already know the stress of getting to work/school and back home each day. Soothing music helps, or simple body exercises that are possible in the confines of a car, listening to a 'talking-book' is an excellent way to pass the time as it's useful and takes your mind off the traffic around you. You're going to be a driver for many years. You may as well learn to take a calm approach to traffic or you'll be an early candidate for stress overload.

Twins

If you are one of a set of twins, you will know that the stress of this has to do with identity. It's fun when you're small to be dressed alike and have everyone make a fuss of you, but when you're a teenager, the very thing you're trying to establish is your individuality. People very seldom talk to one twin without mentioning the other. As you get older, you can be more assertive about this and insist on being treated as a separate person but it's probably difficult now. Don't let the down side spoil your relationship with each other.

Keep the best of being a twin — it's a unique and wonderful bond — but gradually pull away by doing things separately, developing your own interests and dressing differently.

Ugliness/squalor

Studies have shown that the environment in which people work, study and live is very influential in determining lifestyle and stress levels. Very ugly apartment blocks appear to promote crime, domestic violence and depression. Huge sums of money are spent in personalising office buildings with gardens, atriums and the like. I know I can't work in a tiny, cooped-in area without a window, certainly not for long periods, and I need to see greenery outside. I believe very strongly in the therapeutic benefits of nature. So, if you go to a school where all you can see are grey buildings, try to spend some time outside at the end of the day. Don't complain if you have to share a small room at home or your house is not in a pleasant street — get yourself to the nearest body of water and play sport or jog every morning. Remember, it's not the facts of your life that matter, but your approach to those facts. You can brighten up the darkest room with your smile and the ugliest place with the radiance of your enthusiasm.

Venereal disease

There's so much talk about AIDS these days, we've forgotten that there are many other conditions also brought on by sexual contact that should be taken into account when considering intercourse and health risks. One common VD is herpes, and there's also chlamydia. You can find out more about these by getting information pamphlets from the Health Department in your state.

Violence

I specifically want to talk here about violence in the media which is blamed for crime and aggressive behaviour in society. Many studies have been made that show a link between sex and horror videos, movies and television and the violence that goes on in our streets. There should be no confusion in your mind between fantasy and reality if you remember that all human beings have a dark side to their natures. We all crave excitement, the unknown and danger. To deny this is just as unhealthy as indulging it without restraint. Let it out in positive ways and you will be able to stay on the healthy and legal side of life. I'll let you in on a secret — I love horror movies. Never once have I had a violent or anti-social thought as a result of seeing one. You know why? Because I recognise it as a fantasy. I switch off the TV or leave the cinema knowing I have let out some of my negative energies by watching imaginary killers hack away at celluloid victims, and then I totally forget it. You can do the same whether it's scary films or screaming on a roller coaster or hitting a punching bag. Let out your aggressions; don't let them build up, and you'll be right. Of course, I must say again that anything done to excess can be harmful, so try not to use videos and television as a substitute for living.

Weather

Human beings are very affected by the weather, and some of us match our moods to the sunshine or rain. There is even a condition called 'seasonal adjustment disorder', which causes sufferers to experience 'flu symptoms and depression each time the seasons turn around. Bad weather can make us 'blue', sunny weather happy and bright. You may already have noticed this in your life, although not all of you will feel this equally. Really hot weather can be stressful as it saps our energy, makes us irritable and unable to concentrate. The best way to combat ups and downs due to the weather is to stop judging the day by whether it's sunny or wet. Every day is a good day!

Wet dreams/bed-wetting

Wet dreams are very common for teenage boys. It is the name for an ejaculation that occurs during sleep, usually brought on by an erotic dream. There is nothing to be ashamed of. If you have a mother you can talk to, just tell her about it and change the sheets. The same goes for bed-wetting, except that this condition affects both boys and girls. It is not as common or frequent as in younger children but it does happen; in fact, it can happen even in adulthood, as a result of excessive fluid intake before sleep, bladder or kidney infection, or incontinence due to age or a physical problem.

Agencies teenagers can call on

Youth Legal Service
Health Department
Department of Community Services
Commissioner for Equal Opportunity
Drug and Alcohol Authority
Crisis Care
Citizens' Advice Bureau
Salvation Army
Centacare
Anglicare
Family Planning Association
Pregnancy Help
Police Child Abuse Unit
Sexual Abuse Centre
Youth Accommodation Coalition
YMCA
YWCA
National Youthline
Youth Hostels Association
AIDS Council
Youth Affairs Council
Adoption Jigsaw
Alcoholics Anonymous
Al-Anon
Alateen
Allergy Association
Health Promotions
Cancer Foundation
Commonwealth Employment Service
Department of Employment, Education and Training
Career Reference Centre
Consumer Advisory Service
TAFE Information and Counselling Services
Department of Social Security
Marriage Guidance Council
Incest Survivors' Association/Anonymous
Office of the Family
Council of Social Services
Ministry of Education
Legal Aid Commission
Family Court
Australian Taxation Office
Department of Nutrition and Dietetics
Tenants Advice Service

You will need to look for the equivalent to these agencies in your state, if they go by another name (the front of the telephone book is a good place to start).

BOOKS FOR TEENAGERS

RELATING TO OTHERS AS YOU GROW UP

Barbeau, Clayton, *A teenager's survival kit: how to raise parents*, Collins Dove, 1988.

Freed, Alvyn M., *T.A. for teens*, Jalmar Press, 1976.

Hobbs, Amrita, *It could be different: a self-help book for teenagers*, Harmony Holidays, 1991.

Matthews, Andrew, *Being happy*, Media Masters, 1988.

Matthews, Andrew, *Making friends*, Media Masters, 1990.

Montgomery, Bob, and Laurel Morris, *Getting on with the oldies*, Lothian, 1988.

Palmer, Pat, *Teen esteem*, Impact, 1989.

BODY CHANGES AND SEXUALITY

Gale, Jay, and John Porter, *Sexuality: a boy's guide*, McPhee Gribble, 1989.

Gardener-Luolan, Joann, Bonnie Lopez and Marcia Quackenbush, *Period*, Penguin, 1992.

Llewellyn-Jones, Derek, and Suzanne Abrahams, *Everygirl*, Oxford University Press, 1986.

McCloskey, Jenny, *Your sexual health*, Elephas, 1992.

Parsons, A. & I., *Making it from 12 to 20: how to survive your teens*, Penguin, 1988.

Voss, Jacqueline, and Jay Gale, *Sexuality: a girl's guide*, McPhee Gribble, 1989.

Wootten, Vicki, *Be yourself: love, sex and you, a guide for teenagers*, Penguin, 1989.

STUDY SKILLS AND EXAMS

Dixon, Jill, *How to be a successful student without quitting the human race*, Penguin, 1988.

Lang, Binny and Chris, *Your future success: a student's guide to effective study*, Ashwood House, 1990.

Newbegin, Ian, *The Australian study guide*, Information Australia, 1991.

Orr, Fred, *Study skills for successful students*, Allen & Unwin, 1992.

Withers, Graeme, *Tackling that test*, Australian Council for Educational Research, 1991.

JOB-SEEKING ETC

Bisdee, Bob, *Successful job-seeking in the 1990s*, Mandarin, 1992.

Bolles, Richard Nelson, *The 1992 what color is your parachute?: a practical manual for job-hunters and career-changers*, Ten Speed Press, 1992 (annual publication).

Stevens, Paul, *Australian résumé guide: making your job application work*, Worklife, 1990.

Ashenden, Dean, and Sandra Milligan, *Good Universities guide to Australian universities and other higher education institutions*, Mandarin, 1991.

SPECIAL ISSUES

Fletcher, Raffaella, and Peter Mayle, *Dangerous candy*, Corgi, 1990. (Drugs).

Glassock, Geoffrey T., and Louise Rowling, *Learning to grieve: life skills for coping with losses, for high school classes*, Millennium, 1992.

Marsh, Jenny, *Stepping out: incest info for girls*, Millennium, 1988.

Zagdanski, Doris, *Something I've never felt before: how teenagers cope with grief*, Hill of Content, 1990.

72 ■ TEENAGE STRESS

BOOKS FOR PARENTS OF TEENAGERS

Davitz, Lois and Joel, *How to live almost happily with a teenager,* Collins Dove, 1982.

Maxwell, Ruth, *Kids, alcohol and drugs,* Ballantine, 1991.

Montgomery, Bob, and Laurel Morris, *Getting on with your teenagers,* Lothian, 1988.

Murphy, Leola and Eamon, *High school success: how to help your teenager succeed at high school,* Leaf Press, 1990.

Patterson, Gerald, and Marion Forgatch, *Parents and adolescents living together: part 1, the basics,* 1987; *part 2, family problem solving,* 1989; Castalia Publishing.

Weinhaus, Evonne, and Karen Friedman, *Stop struggling with your teenager,* McPhee Gribble, 1987.

Agencies teenagers can call on

Youth Legal Service
Health Department
Department of Community
  Services
Commissioner for Equal
  Opportunity
Drug and Alcohol Authority
Crisis Care
Citizens' Advice Bureau
Salvation Army
Centacare
Anglicare
Family Planning Association
Pregnancy Help
Police Child Abuse Unit
Sexual Abuse Centre
Youth Accommodation
  Coalition
YMCA
YWCA
National Youthline
Youth Hostels Association
AIDS Council
Youth Affairs Council
Adoption Jigsaw
Alcoholics Anonymous

Al-Anon
Alateen
Allergy Association
Health Promotions
Cancer Foundation
Commonwealth Employment
  Service
Department of Employment,
  Education and Training
Career Reference Centre
Consumer Advisory Service
TAFE Information and Coun-
  selling Services
Department of Social Security
Marriage Guidance Council
Incest Survivors' Association/
  Anonymous
Office of the Family
Council of Social Services
Ministry of Education
Legal Aid Commission
Family Court
Australian Taxation Office
Department of Nutrition and
  Dietetics
Tenants Advice Service

You will need to look for the equivalent to these agencies in your state, if they go by another name (the front of the telephone book is a good place to start).

70 ■ TEENAGE STRESS

Your children are life's gift to you, no matter how much they might drive you crazy at times. You can have a terrific relationship. Some of you will have to work harder at this than others. There is no guarantee that you and your children will like each other just because you're related. But over and above your blood ties is the potential for you to relate as people. For this, you need to put aside all the preconceived ideas of what your relationship should be like, and the stereotyped images of happy family relations. There is no real-life 'Brady Bunch' or 'Leave it to Beaver'. We're all just imperfect human beings struggling to connect and to be happy.

Louise Hay, author of the classic, *You Can Heal Your Life*, says we're all 'victims of victims', passing the same hurts down from generation to generation. Only love and awareness can change this.

As the line from the song says, 'Teach your children well.' That's finally all you can really do.

Only as high as I reach can I grow.
Only as far as I seek can I go.
Only as deep as I look can I see.
Only as much as I dream can I be.

KAREN RIVEN

PERSONAL GROWTH ■ 69

First, you worry about their health and welfare when they're growing up, then you have to live through the terrible teens, then they leave home and you worry if they're looking after themselves, then they marry and it all starts again with your grandkids! Of course, there's a tremendous amount of joy along the way, and you wouldn't want it any differently.

Ultimately, however, peace of mind is an individual pursuit and only comes as a result of living, experiencing and learning. What I have tried to give your teenagers in this book is a guide to a happier and more positive life. My message is threefold:

■ The teenagers are responsible for themselves and their own choices, mistakes, triumphs, feelings and actions.
■ They can choose to live their lives more positively.
■ They can reduce stress simply by understanding its nature and learning how to manage it and harness it for good.

When all is said and done, your job as parent was largely done by the time you sent them off to school for the first time. You've just been building on that relationship since then. I saw this process quite clearly when I was a high school teacher. When I taught a class of girls for three years, they would be totally 'mine' in year 8, break all the rules in year 9, and by year 10 they were no longer under my influence. Boys, make-up, clothes and parties had taken my place as the most important component in their lives outside their families. They still loved me but I was now separate from them, not God-like or infallible, just a teacher they would come to occasionally for a chat, some advice or a laugh.

This is how it must be whenever we love young people. If we try to hold on to the past relationship and refuse to adapt, we spoil the beauty of love given freely. Your teenagers are truly wonderful, free, honest and individual. Respect and treasure these qualities in them. Like homing pigeons, they will come back to you if your heart and your arms are open. No, they will not be the same children who were totally dependent on you, and they won't want you to tell them how they should do things or live their lives, but they will always need your approval, and your love.

68 ■ TEENAGE STRESS

behind to live her own life. This dream was Robyn's declaration of her freedom; the final link with her mother's domination was broken.

Sometimes, dreams take on a sinister tone and content, and we call them nightmares. No doubt you have had to comfort your children many times over the years when they've experienced frightening dreams. By the time they reach the teenage years and adulthood, their childish monsters have either disappeared or changed shape. Now, they have different demons to battle — but they can be just as real.

Nightmares are only a problem if the same one recurs to the point where your teenager dreads going to sleep. In these cases, see a doctor and ask for a referral to a dream therapist for your child. Soothing music at bedtime, a relaxation or meditation tape to fall asleep to, some light exercise before getting into bed, a warm drink or taking a dream protector to bed will all help.

Once, a woman rang me on a radio programme to ask about her baby who was sleeping very poorly and waking up screaming every night. The baby seemed terrified even to be put in her cot, and the distraught mother didn't know whether to keep picking her up or leave her to cry. There was a relatively simple answer in this case. It turned out that the baby had just come out of a short stay in hospital. It was obvious that she was still traumatised by the experience and associated her cot with the hospital bed. This was causing the nightmares. My suggestion to the mother was to introduce the idea of the 'dream weapon', despite the child's age, and to stay in the room until she fell asleep, as a short-term measure.

Inner peace

To be at peace with ourselves and the world around us is the greatest gift any human being can possess. I certainly wish it for all my readers. As parents, much of your peace of mind, or lack of it, is tied up with the happiness of your children.

PERSONAL GROWTH ■ 67

as a tragedy. You can help with the learning and rehearsing and then, be a support player during the performance.

Dreams and nightmares

Dreams are a doorway to the subconscious workings of the mind and, therefore, are a rich source of information. It takes time and practice to remember dreams consistently and in detail. It also takes a strong desire. Using a set method of recording is helpful, and studying the dream symbols and messages is essential if the dreamer is to 'read' the images with some accuracy. Dream research has made great strides in the last decade and seemingly incredible things are being achieved. For the ordinary person, the benefit of this expanded knowledge is that we can understand better the nature of sleep, dream activity and the link between our waking and dream lives.

Dreams can actually help us in very practical ways. Take the story of a woman who came in to see me for counselling. Her problem was stress brought on by repressed anger over many years. As a child, she had felt very rejected by her mother. She felt hurt and angry but was never able to let those feelings out. If she was 'naughty' her mother would leave her alone, and make her feel abandoned. When she grew up, her mother still dominated her through her choice of men. She criticised her men friends, and although she married twice, they were not successful marriages. Later in life, when her mother was dying, Robyn met and married a third man, once again against her mother's wishes. Shortly after, her mother died, leaving her daughter a terrible legacy of guilt. When Robyn came in to see me, she was very stressed after a lifetime of grappling with these feelings. Through working together, she gradually released some of the anger and came to understand the issues involved. One night, she dreamt that she was at her mother's bedside as she lay dying. In the dream, she said goodbye clearly to her mother, telling her that she must go and leave Robyn

Suicide

Depression, if unchecked over a long period, can lead to thoughts of suicide. It's not hard to see why, as depression is so depressing! It makes the sufferer want to give up on life, and for teenagers, the daily struggle is already great. Without the mental and physical resources to cope, it all gets too painful, and the idea of opting out begins to look attractive. The main reasons for teenage suicide are:

- Persistent, high levels of stress
- The loss of a loved one, such as the death of a parent or being dumped by a friend
- Feelings of inferiority and inadequacy
- An inability to communicate and relate to others
- Family conflict, especially if it involves alcohol and/or violence
- Not being allowed to have something that is obsessively desired; for example, boys and girls forbidden to date or see each other have suicided together, as Romeo and Juliet did

Underlying all these is a dreadful aloneness, for every suicide is based on the belief that 'nobody cares'. Some teenagers may really be reaching out for help by swallowing those pills or slashing their wrists — a desperate cry for someone to notice their pain. Others make a cold, calculated decision to end their lives because they simply no longer want the pain and the struggle.

You can't help your children once they've passed this point, but you have an irreplaceable role to play in prevention. Even the most loving, accepting and generous parents can be faced with a teenager on drugs, on the streets or on the mortuary slab. For me to suggest that you shouldn't feel responsible or guilty because your children have made these decisions for themselves would be pointless. However, this analogy may help: you are one of the leading players in the drama of your child's life, but he or she is the star. You cannot blame yourself if lines are forgotten, scenes spoiled and the story finishes up

Depression notes

Factors controlling Depression
- Stress
- Coping strategies
- Self-image
- Focus of the anxiety
- Self-generating worry
- Insecurity/self doubt

Symptoms
- Irritability
- Insomnia
- Inability to relax
- Inability to concentrate
- Crying
- Dependence
- Withdrawal
- Inertia/Lethargy

Strategies to handle Depression
- Action
- Breathing space/distancing/centring
- Willingness to change
- Faith and positive thinking
- Physical health
- Attitude
- Share your problem
- Letting go
- Make a list of things that make you happy
- Make a list of things that make you unhappy
- Diminish the negative; emphasise the positive. What do want from life?
- Unhappiness, though undesirable, is still comfortable, so take a chance on change

Of course, long-term depression may require medical intervention, as there could be a biological cause or drug therapy may be needed to stem the condition.

64 ■ TEENAGE STRESS

negative thinking?
- Replacing the negative with the positive
- Positive thinking linked directly to self-esteem and confidence
- The role of identity in positive thinking
- Mind power
- Don't control — reshape!
- Fear and doubt — our two worst enemies
- Fear is a fantasy
- Self-image and signals; body language
- The mind and disease
- Intuition and the 'inner you'

Depression

The opposite to positive thinking is depression, and, unfortunately, there are more depressed than positive teenagers around. The mind doesn't make any value judgements. Its power can be directed towards the negative and the positive equally. To complicate things even further, depression is more than a mental condition although it may begin as such. It can result from a chemical imbalance, hormonal fluctuations or prolonged stress. Therefore, there is absolutely no point in telling your teenager to 'snap out of it' when you see him or her depressed.

The odd day of feeling down is par for the course, but chronic depression is potentially serious. The best way to deal with it is to observe for a while and see if you can identify the cause, such as an ongoing problem at school. Be very careful not to overreact or place undue pressure, as a depressed person cannot always think rationally or give coherent answers. If there is a reasonable explanation for the sadness and unhappiness, help where you can; just being around and available to listen is probably the best lifeline you can offer.

Here are some common symptoms of depression and useful techniques for dealing with it.

world we now inhabit, I don't think young people have that luxury anymore. They need every advantage in order to get jobs, have healthy relationships and stay on top of emotional chaos.

Mind power, like so many other life-skills, has to be practised on a daily basis. It is a conscious decision to harness mental energy and turn it from negative to positive. This can be done by saying positive affirmations, studying and reading about the power of the mind, meditation, choosing from moment to moment to think positively. I believe it is a vital tool for teenagers, although they're unlikely to be very good at it because of their immaturity, lack of life-experience, and low self-confidence. It's one of life's many contradictions that those who would benefit most from positive thinking also find it the most difficult.

That's where you come in. Your example is crucial. If your teenager comes in from a job interview focusing on the negative aspects, you can say, 'I suppose you blew it again!' or 'I'm sure you did okay. Tell me about it.' Multiply this by the hundreds of times each day when you are presented with the opportunity to either lift your teenager up or crush his/her spirit. I used to feel that my mother didn't support me because she always assumed I was wrong. If I came home from school and said I got yelled at, she would immediately say, 'What did you do?' As an adult, I can see that she was a practical person and simply wanted to get to the heart of the matter, but, as a child, I longed to be held and comforted, even if I was wrong. Your teenagers desperately need your positive responses, even if you have to pretend to feel them sometimes.

Listed below are some general points about positive thinking that may help you:

Positive thinking

- Not unrealistic, false happiness; but an attitude, a way of life
- Happiness as an integral part of living, not a fixed goal
- How do I start thinking positively, after perhaps years of

62 ■ TEENAGE STRESS

— a backlash of fear disguised as hatred. If you love your children, you will encourage them to open their minds and their hearts to all types of people and experiences. You can't keep them safe by keeping them ignorant.

Spirituality embraces the concept that human beings are more than flesh and bone; we also have an eternal, unseen aspect, and this needs nurturing as much as the physical part. Apart from religious worship, our spiritual hunger can be satisfied by fine music, art, conversation, poetry, love and sharing, friendship and family, nature and animals.

Of course, some of you may be non-religious and have religious children! This is less common, but if it's the scenario in your family you need the same amount of tolerance as religious parents who find themselves with a teenager who's an atheist or a Hare Krishna or a crystal-gazing, chanting astrologer! True love sees past these differences, through to the beautiful person within.

Mind power

This is the new 'religion' for the 90s. So much has been written and spoken about it in the last few decades that millions of people around the world today live by its principles. Has it any real validity, and how can it help your children?

When you think that each of us has literally thousands of thoughts on any given day, we can programme our lives for disappointments, setbacks and problems if most of these thoughts are negative. This is based on the belief that as we think, so we act and feel. Naturally, you want your teenagers to succeed in the world, and the two killers to their efforts will be negative thinking ('I'm never going to get a job') and low self-esteem ('I'm not good at anything').

That's why I believe that it's important for them to make choices about their attitudes early in life. Many people live and die without tapping the enormous potential that lies beneath the surface of their own existences. In the complex

PERSONAL GROWTH ■ 61

your teenager will get. I can only suggest you lighten the pressure as much as possible, even if you feel very strongly about it. You are within your rights to insist that your children go with you to church, especially while they're living at home — but what is the point if there is no personal faith or conviction?

It comes back to trusting the job you've done as parents up to now. If you've trained your children in spiritual matters and set a good example, that's all you can do. The rest is up to them and God. The approach of some parents to religion is the same as the approach of some parents to show business — obsessive and pushy. This may work when your children are small, but continue to try it on with teenagers and you'll push them away. They're going to be much more influenced by your beliefs if they see you living them. Sunday Christianity is unlikely to impress them, and they'll probably tell you so!

Spirituality

While your teenagers may choose not to follow a traditionally religious path, they're always going to be spiritual beings. Understanding their spiritual natures is a lifelong challenge for them. They might simply choose to follow a different religion or they may go down a different path altogether. If they come to you and say they're interested in metaphysics or New Age teachings, are you going to pronounce these studies to be the work of the devil because you don't understand them? So much conflict in relationships stems from ignorance. As broadminded as I like to think I am, I can remember a time in my life when I was threatened by anything unfamiliar to me — homosexuality, black people, 'way-out' religions, just to name a few.

New ideas can be the most threatening thing in the world, because they push us out of our comfort zones and force us to consider different ways of thinking and acting. A common reaction is to strike out in anger, and we see this happening every day of the week in towns and cities around the world

8 Personal Growth

This chapter, in many ways, rounds off the book's message and summarises some of the key issues. It deals with an area that you're likely to have strong views about, and I don't expect you to agree with me on many of the topics raised.

Religion

Religion, for example, is a highly emotive subject that wars have been fought over. So it's usually best to avoid talking about it if at all possible. Everyone has an opinion on religion, whether for or against, and it's a subject that people rarely discuss unemotionally. However, I didn't see any way that I could avoid bringing it up in a chapter about personal development.

Those of you who are religious in the traditional sense will naturally want your teenagers to follow in your footsteps. This is akin to the point made about family occupational histories. At first, your teenager's refusal to attend church and their questioning of your church's teachings and rules can be put down to natural rebellion. This is a major turning-point, however, as views formed now might influence their worshipping patterns for the years to come. As with so many other principles, the more insistent you are, the more stubborn

WORK AND EMPLOYMENT ■ 59

a buffer between them and the realities of life. Soon enough they'll take their full place in society. Let them lean a bit for the time being. At the same time, avoid smothering them with too much protection. Walk a little distance behind but be there. Their motivation to succeed or to fail was planted years ago, but it's not fixed in stone. You can still help them take a more positive approach to themselves and to life's opportunities, in whatever practical and emotional ways you can. There are more tips on this in the next chapter.

58 ■ TEENAGE STRESS

take her medicine, but if they treated her like a child, how could she ever regain their trust? Wouldn't it be better to take charge of her own money and prove that she could be responsible? Obviously, if she failed again, they could still enforce total control.

Budgeting should be kept as simple as possible for teenagers. If you are prepared to teach them the rudiments of banking, taxation and money management, great; if not, professional advice can be sought. Then, it's up to your teenager to take over, especially if he/she no longer lives at home. Advise them strongly to pay for essentials first, to shop carefully — particularly in supermarkets, which are traps for the unwary — and to save a little every week. Beyond that, you have to trust them to manage. As they get older, and start to want information about larger purchases, funds for travel, investing money and the like, they will hopefully come to you for guidance, and you can point them in the right direction if you don't know the answers.

Success

Success means different things to different people. As parents, you undoubtedly want your children to be happy, fulfilled and secure. They have to find their own road to these things, and you have to watch them fail and falter over and over again, just as you watched them struggle to take their first steps all those years ago. You couldn't walk for them then and you can't succeed for them now. Perhaps, after all, that is the greatest test of love: that we love our children enough to let them go, and yet be there for them when we're needed. The 'If you don't do what I tell you, you can just leave and don't bother coming back' approach is very destructive for everyone concerned. 'I told you so' isn't much better. You're *supposed* to know more than your children, that's a given, but they need to make their own mistakes and learn their own lessons.

In matters of work, as in everything else, your love can be

WORK AND EMPLOYMENT ■ 57

As a practical way to stave off the unemployment blues, encourage your teenager to take the courses that the CES runs, check out all job opportunities in the local area, and keep busy and active. With the right attitude and sustained effort, a job, however humble, *can* be found. And with each job comes a new opportunity, increased self-respect and another entry for the resumé. Thus out of little acorns do large oaks grow.

Money

Handling money is one of the first social skills your child learns, but there's a vast difference between pocket money spent or banked weekly and budgeting for life's necessities. I always advise parents to teach their children fiscal responsibilities early in life. This is no different from sex education, table manners or getting along with others. What they learn from you in the family arena essentially stays with them for life. If they see you spending money in an extravagant way, they'll either lean towards the same behaviour or go to the other extreme. From the time you start doling out pocket money, there are choices to be made — spend or save, purchase this item or save up and buy something else, and so on. Your opinion will be sought, especially when they're younger, and one hopes that, by the time they're teenagers, they have a reasonable idea what is required to budget money.

Too much control is as harmful as too little. A girl of eighteen wrote to my column with this story: her parents had bought her a car and she had moved in with a girlfriend. One night, she had too much to drink and crashed the car, also incurring trouble with the law. Her parents had insisted the girl return home, pay back the money for the car and hand over all her banking to her parents. They completely removed all control for the girl's financial responsibilities from her hands. Some of this arrangement was imposed by the court but they went too far, in my opinion. My advice to the girl was to tell her parents that she'd learnt her lesson, that she was prepared to

56 ■ TEENAGE STRESS

months of humiliating rejection and defeat. I counsel young people who find themselves in this situation to stay confident, to keep trying and to believe in their own dreams. That's a pretty tall order when you hear remarks like the following day after day: 'You've got nothing to offer; go and get some experience then I might think about hiring you'; 'I can choose from hundreds of hopefuls, why should I pick you?'

If your teenager is determined to find work, remember that it *is* possible but it requires tenacity and resilience, qualities not usually strong in teenagers, so your support is vital. If you keep nagging your son or daughter to find work, ridiculing them if they fail at interviews and being negative about their chances, you could be spoiling their hopes for the future. Stay positive yourself even if you don't always feel it, and encourage your child to improve skills, keep writing job applications and consider all job options. What may start off as a low job choice could end up perfect for your teenager. The same applies to unpaid volunteer work, which can sometimes become a paid job. It's a fine line between being too fussy and settling for whatever's offering.

In job hunting, being prepared is essential. Encourage your teenager to make sure they have a thorough resumé, a professional attitude, and persistence in looking for work, sending applications and attending interviews.

Unemployment and your teenager

Coping with chronic unemployment is extremely damaging to the self-esteem. That's true even of seasoned workers with years of successful employment under their belts, so how much more true is it for teenagers? That's why your patience and understanding are so crucial. If a teenager is genuinely trying to find work, he/she should be given every opportunity to succeed without being labelled a dole-bludger or put down for taking too long to get a job. Of course, some may be lazy or apathetic but they need encouragement, not criticism.

WORK AND EMPLOYMENT ■ 55

it may be necessary to research other possibilities if your child has no particular profession in mind. Those teenagers who are clear about what they want to do in life are far luckier, even if you don't like their choice.

Choosing a career is a very important step for this age-group as the right selection means job satisfaction and, hopefully, financial security, while the wrong one can cause years of bitterness. That's why it's crucial that you don't exert your influence unduly.

Tertiary studies

Once your teenager has decided what to do, achieving it is the next challenge. If it's continuing into tertiary education, your practical assistance may be required by way of financial support, helping with accommodation, textbooks, transport, and assistance with the academic aspect as well because most university students fail and/or drop out in the first year. Encouragement, providing a tutor if you can afford it, creating a suitable learning environment, laying down a few ground rules for study — all these can be useful support systems.

Helping your teenager get a job

Perhaps the hardest road to pick in this economic time is to enter the job market. If a student has no plans for an academic career, and is uninterested in a trade or apprenticeship, going straight out to work is about the only other choice. In our day, that was as easy as filling in an application form, but that's all changed. Your teenager will be competing with thousands of other unskilled young people. The only thing that will make a difference is having a competitive edge. This may take the form of a professional resumé, or a special skill that's considered desirable in the job market, or a very personable and enthusiastic approach. Without it, your teenager could face

7 Work and Employment

The matter of your teenager's future job prospects, employment, success and financial stability is bound to be of vital importance to you. Unfortunately, it is also an area of potential stress and conflict, especially if there is disagreement between you and your child about the basics. You may have a specific desire to see your son or daughter as a lawyer, for instance, perhaps because there's a history of lawyers in the family, or you may want your teenager to follow in your chosen profession or field, whatever it may be. This is fine if it also happens to be what your child wants, but in most cases, teenagers have ideas of their own and feel very pressured to conform to their parents' wishes. The most loving way to approach this problem is to guide, counsel, advise but not tell, demand or force.

Helping with career choice

There are many ways in which you can help your teenager to find the best career path to suit his or her needs, personality, intelligence level, personal tastes, and so on. Working with the school is a good idea — attend parents' nights, stay involved with the progress of your teenager's school achievements, be prepared to talk about choices, options and requirements for different jobs and careers. As school-leaving time approaches,

HEALTH ■ 53

all, randy teenage boys and overweight teenage girls have always been around.

Exercise is one possible remedy for imbalanced hormonal and biological states. Excess emotional and physical energy can be successfully channelled through running, swimming and team sports. These also teach fitness, coordination, competitiveness and fair play. It's important, however, that you don't pressure your able teenagers to win, win, win, or ridicule your less able offspring. Many parents seek to achieve success and glory through their children's efforts. This is a major area of stress for teenagers, whether it be in the sporting, scholastic or personal arena. Encouragement and support are vital, in the form of attending sports days, helping with training, pep talks, buying the necessary gear and so on, but pushing and demanding specific results is very harmful and can lead to many of the unhealthy states we've talked about in this chapter.

Good health is not just a matter of staying virus, infection or disease free. It implies a whole mental attitude and way of life. The foundation you help your teenagers to build now will hold them in good stead for the rest of their lives.

52 ■ TEENAGE STRESS

in a parent with that attitude, and you can't help or prevent if you don't know what's happening. There are many avenues of help available once you have the facts. If you are open and loving and refuse to condemn, you ought never to lose your child to drugs or alcohol or homelessness or chronic unemployment, because you have given them a foundation of love and trust that will see them through the many storms of life.

Once young people are hooked, it's very hard for them to get off. Drugs have many faces, and if teenagers learn to reach for the bottle, the tablet or the syringe to fix their problems, to heal their hurts and to mask their frustrations, they will do it all their lives. In chapter 8, I will examine ways and means to replace these negative dependencies with positive solutions.

Diet and exercise

If you have a teenage daughter, watch for eating disorders as they are extremely common in this age-group and females are more prone. The signs are easy to detect: extreme thinness, physical deterioration, lethargy, obsession about food, loss of appetite. Overweight overeaters also need to be watched carefully as this is simply a different form of the same problem. Denial is a major factor in these conditions, so just asking your teenager if she is a sufferer or pressing her to eat or stop eating so much, whichever the case may be, will not work. Medical intervention and/or counselling is required, so refuse to take no for an answer and get your child help without delay.

As with drug-taking and alcohol consumption, eating disorders often mask a psychological problem, usually an exaggerated version of the teenage condition with all its insecurities, confusion and extreme emotions. It's arguable that teenage boys use sex to deal with their frustrations about life in general and girls use food. If either of these becomes so excessive as to be out of control, you need to intervene; otherwise, it can just form part of the growing-up process. After

Drugs

These constitute a very serious social problem, and it would be foolish to suggest that the solution lies in the hands of any individual or group in the community. The reasons for drug-taking and addiction are many and varied. Some, unfortunately, trace back to the home and family influences. Drug-taking often stems from unhappiness, extreme stress conditions and self-dislike. As much as teenagers experience these emotions in the domestic environment, parents are targetted for blame when young people leave home and/or get into drugs. I'd love to suggest that all you need to do to stamp out drug addiction in the community is to provide a loving, stable place for your children, not just in the physical place but emotionally as well. Unfortunately, that's too simplistic an answer as teenagers who get hooked on heroin or cocaine or even marijuana don't only come from broken homes or disturbed families.

Obviously, there are other factors involved in the drug problem of the 90s. We need to give our young people a sense of purpose in this unstable, sometimes frightening world. Every generation blames the previous one for the flawed world it has inherited, yet we keep making the same mistakes. Teenagers today seem to have less hope and optimism than ever before, especially in the area of material well-being. How can we ask them to stay sober and drug-free if the world appears to have nothing for them? Some are emotionally stronger and can weather the disappointments and difficulties at school and when they move into the outside world. Others, who are perhaps more sensitive or lacking in confidence or psychologically vulnerable, can be easily led into experimenting with dangerous substances and may be hooked before they even understand what it means.

What can you as a parent do? Educate yourselves. Don't ever hide from unpleasant truths or refuse to consider unpalatable possibilites. The 'it can't happen to my child' approach is very dangerous because a teenager in trouble is unlikely to confide

50 ■ TEENAGE STRESS

the role of liquor in your home. Is it used purely as a social, recreational substance? Is it used always in moderation and within reasonable limits? Do you ever have guests in your home who drink to excess and display behaviour that is out of control? Do you as parents ever allow alcohol to influence your actions and words, especially in relation to your children?

You are role-models for your children and when they are teenagers, they have already learnt their lessons well. Therefore, if you demand, for instance, that they refrain from drinking alcohol, you have to ensure that you live by the same rule. If they have seen you regularly abuse the use of liquor, they will brand you as hypocritical and take no notice of your instructions. Respect has to be earned and forged over many years — it can never be freely given if simply demanded.

Young people generally do not accept the argument that they have to abide by separate rules because they are the children and you are the parents. I'm not a great lover of black and white rules, anyway. If, for religious or health reasons, you would prefer your teenagers not to drink at all, you can ask them to respect your wishes at home until they're past the age of legal alcohol consumption. However, that puts a great burden of stress on them to please you, and if they can't abide by your rules, they end up sneaking around and perhaps overdoing it instead of handling alcohol maturely.

Alcohol is not evil in itself. If it's used sensibly, it can be a pleasurable adjunct to an evening's entertainment. It's dangerous if it becomes the main focus of social activities and if it's taken to excess. Why not preach moderation? Let your teenagers have an occasional beer at home or a glass of wine with dinner. Teach them interesting facts about wine-making, the different types of beer, how to mix light cocktails. It can be fun and informative and, best of all, in this way alcohol loses its mystique. When things are forbidden, they immediately take on a more desirable aspect, so approach with as light a touch as possible in this and other areas.

Of course, if your teenager shows signs of alcohol dependence, seek professional help.

HEALTH · ■ 49

Education and prevention are the key weapons in this fight, and the best way for you to provide support and help is to stay in touch with your teenager's emotions, problems and needs.

Smoking

Many of you smoke yourselves, and you probably wish that you hadn't got addicted to cigarettes when you were teenagers. This may cause you to come down a bit too hard on your youngsters if you catch them experimenting in this area. But if they've seen you smoking all the time they've been growing up, they're not going to listen when you insist that they shouldn't start. If you're non-smokers, it still won't be easy to convince your kids not to try cigarettes if all their friends are doing it.

You'd be wise to speak honestly to your children, pre-teenage, about this. Tell them that you know they're going to be under pressure to try smoking, advise them of the pitfalls and health risks, and then say you'd rather they didn't start at all but if they must give it a go, you don't want them sneaking around to do it. This removes the guilt aspect and pays respect to their own choices over their bodies. If they smoke at home or around the house, at least you can monitor the frequency without being too obvious about it.

Beyond this, you can't do much more to stop your teenagers smoking short of forbidding them, which would only increase their desire to go ahead. I certainly recommend that you do whatever you can to stop them getting hooked on smoking because tobacco is a very addictive drug and habits formed now might stay as health hazards in your teenagers' lives permanently. Seek advice and guidance from the Department of Health and the Drug and Alcohol Authority, if necessary.

Alcohol

As with adults, teenagers often turn to alcohol in times of stress. The first important thing you need to do is to examine honestly

6 Health

As parents, you no doubt care a lot about your teenagers' health. Since your children were small, you've tried to feed them well, make sure they get enough sleep, are warmly dressed, exercise sufficiently, etc. As they got older, they probably told you to stop fussing, that they were old enough to take care of themselves. It's much easier to care for a little baby who's completely dependent on you than a teenager who resents your efforts, yet in many ways, your teenagers are just as vulnerable in the world, although they may be less helpless. Life holds more subtle dangers now, and in this chapter, I shall go through some of the more insidious ones that can affect your children.

Emotion and stress

In chapter 1, the link between stress and health was discussed. If a teenager is living with undue amounts of stress, whether emotional or physical, good health is eroded away. Many pointers have been given throughout the book to enable you to gauge the stress levels of your children. If you notice any persistent warning signs, try to establish the precise nature of the problem; discuss the causes, symptoms and strategies for change that suit your home life and the personality and schedule of your teenager.

EMOTIONS ■ 47

they are to do with schoolwork, addictions, health problems, low self-esteem, sexuality, family conflicts. Need I say then that they need your help in this area more than in any other? Even a lot of their negative behaviour is a cry for help, a scream for attention. We see this clearly with very small children, who will often put on a turn if Mum is busy and cannot offer undivided attention. This dies down as the child grows but can rear its ugly head again during teenage, only instead of whingeing and crying, they might take drugs or commit crimes.

You can't shield them from living their lives, in fact it would be quite wrong for you to try, but you can act as a buffer for them, not only while they're in your home and your care but all their lives, as long as you're around. And if you've done the job right, they'll be strong enough after you've gone to get on with it and teach their children in turn.

46 ■ TEENAGE STRESS

and accepted. Animals are seen being born and, when they're old or slaughtered, they die. In families where three or more generations live together, the progress from birth to death is obvious.

It's only when we hide from the less pleasant truths of our existence that they become frightening. If the fact of death is never acknowledged, and then it suddenly hits, maybe in the form of a schoolmate, neighbour or an aged relative dying, it's very shocking to a child, because death is an abstract, the ultimate unknown. It can't be explained in human terms because no-one has ever come back to describe it for us. Now, with the instances of what is known as 'clinical death' or 'near-death experience', we are piecing together a better understanding of what it might be like. There's no need, however, to use the laws of metaphysics to explain to children about the spirit. All major religions teach about the existence of an eternal soul, and some Eastern religions believe in reincarnation, which is a theory of multiple lifetimes for each spirit-being.

After the loss of a loved one, and when the initial period of mourning has passed, a teenager is much more inclined to listen to a sensible argument than a patronising talk about how wonderful death is and how much better it is in Heaven. As a child, I remember wondering why, if a dead person had 'gone to God', his family were all standing at the graveside wailing and weeping. Now I understand these contradictions, but we need to always put ourselves into the mind of a confused child before we tell them things.

When my mother died, the family, in well-meaning ignorance, shielded my small brother and sister from the facts. I remember that they played ball in the garden on the day of her death and I wondered if they knew she'd gone. Older relatives assured me it was best for them to be left out of the grief process. But they were never given a chance to cry for her and, therefore, never resolved the loss.

If you consider all the problems that your teenagers live with and tackle every day, they are all emotionally based, whether

EMOTIONS ■ 45

them and think, 'Oh my God, I haven't done things that way. I've ruined my child's life.' Of course you haven't. Imperfection is to be embraced: it's what makes us all wonderful, human, learning beings. Is there anything more boring than a 'perfect' person?

Death and loss

One other emotional area I need to talk about before we leave this chapter is loss. Teenagers are always in the throes of losing something, whether it's friends, marks at school, their patience, their bags, you name it, but when it comes to serious loss, such as the death of a parent, the damage leaves a permanent scar. In this day of unusual family combinations, it's almost the exception for young people to have two parents and brothers and sisters. But security doesn't come in the form of convention. Kids don't much care who looks after them as long as they feel loved. It's when a beloved carer disappears that a child's world is shattered. Sometimes people go away; sometimes they are taken away, as in the case of illness and/ or death. Then, a child feels abandoned and can spend its whole life seeking the childhood love that was lost. If your family has been through this type of tragedy, you'll know what I'm talking about.

Yet, as a society, we can help children and teenagers to deal with these losses better. If you are a religious family, you can talk to them about life after death, and going to a better place, but this will only be effective at certain ages. A very small child understands only that its mummy or daddy has gone; a teenager will possibly greet the loss of a parent with anger at God, the surviving parent or even the dead one. Also, as discussed earlier, there'll be irrational guilt. A child might blame itself for a parent's death, no matter how unlikely that may be. Death is a natural process and, like sex, should be talked about freely in the home. On farms and in the country generally, where life is more basic, the cycle of life and death is readily visible

44 ■ TEENAGE STRESS

et cetera, you will cause unnecessary confusion. You won't always agree and your children will play you off against each other, but make up your minds early in the piece who's going to decide what and stick to it.

Continuity is also crucial. It's no good being overly strict one day and indulgent the next. As you are human, you won't be exactly the same all the time, but the world is such an inconstant place, it would be nice if your teenagers could rely on security and safety at least at home.

Keep lines of communication open. Let your teenagers feel safe to speak their minds freely instead of demanding honesty and then coming down like a ton of bricks if you don't like what you hear. Give time for exchange — never be too busy to listen, even if you have to create a space in your day for talk and love. Ask them about their interests.

Be honest and frank. If you say to your teenager, 'I feel really rotten today. I'm sorry I spoke harshly to you earlier', that makes you human. Your teenagers may prefer you to be perfect beings but they'll appreciate your honesty more. What they won't respect is blustering, posturing, covering up your faults, blaming them for everything, not accepting your own failures, and being unable to say you're sorry. You are a parent, not a taskmaster. You can be candid about their faults if you are prepared to own up to your own.

If they can't have or do something, try to avoid the 'because I say so' approach. They will accept your decision better if you offer a reason. Say right away if the answer is no to something rather than 'we'll see', which would have to be in the top ten hate-phrases of things that parents say.

Love, praise and respect them. Yes, they have a right to your respect just because you brought them here. They don't have to do anything to earn it and if you make them feel they do, they will never learn to love themselves. Disagreeing and even arguing and quarrelling is quite healthy as long as it takes place in a spirit of love.

These are the main skills you can practise, but don't read

EMOTIONS ■ 43

a child feels, the less anxious the teenager and adult. Personality factors have also to be taken into account. Some children and teenagers are, by nature, more anxious, more eager to please and more self-disciplined. You know if this applies to yours. If it does, your role as reinforcer can work for or against this tendency. In other words, your responses and reactions will either feed the anxiety or soothe away the doubts. Of course, you yourself could be a nervous, over-zealous person, so be aware that you are a constant model for your children.

By the time they are teenagers, they are quite likely to want to do the opposite of what you do but they can't unlearn the lessons overnight. If you make a big deal of everything, so will they; if you are a worrier, they may adopt this method of dealing with their problems; if you are very hard on yourself, they will probably follow suit. It's very seldom that I work with a teenager and cannot see the same problem(s) in the parent(s).

Some anxiety is normal, especially with the complexity of life in the 90s, but too much causes the kind of stress that is very harmful, as we saw in chapter 1.

Very often, one parent is the anxious one and the other calmer and more placid. This should, in theory, provide a balance for the children, but it can, instead, create conflict: Mum says anything goes, Dad demands strict rules in the house to be adhered to, or Dad is the one to go to for indulgence, Mum's got a short fuse and can't deal with upsets. This sets up tremendous confusion in a home unless there's an unusual level of honest communication and everyone can laugh at themselves. But we know from statistics and news stories, that family life is a place of torture and uncertainty and emotional pain for a lot of young people. Good parenting skills are, therefore, vital.

Parenting skills

Unity is the most important parenting skill. If you are not unified in your approach to rules in the home, concessions,

42 ■ TEENAGE STRESS

in families. Teenagers have already internalised years of guilt over all the things they've done wrong since birth. They wear the guilt of causing their mother's pain in childbirth, wearing their parents out as babies, costing heaps of money via their need for clothes, schooling, toys, outings, etc., being 'naughty', disappointing their parents in a thousand ways; and so the sad list continues.

You might be thinking that you've never made your child feel guilty in these ways but remember, guilt isn't rational. You don't have to say to your child, 'You cost us a lot of money' or 'You make us tired, having to look after you all the time'. When you say you're tired, a child will automatically take it personally. That's just the natural egocentricity of youth.

One of the worst examples of guilt misplaced on a child's shoulders is in the case of conflict between its parents. When you quarrel, a child assumes it's to blame. If you separate or divorce, a child will ask itself, 'What did I do?' I have counselled adults whose parents divorced when they were children or teenagers and they still carry the guilt. They almost seem surprised when I suggest that they had nothing to do with their parents' problems, and will protest, 'But I must have been naughty' or 'My parents didn't love me'.

The things you can do to counteract the destructive effects of guilt are: give lots of praise; tell your teenagers when you're angry with them and, most importantly, why; always add the 'I love you' after criticism so that they don't get into their heads that disapproval equals a loss of love; be as positive as possible in the way you speak to and about them; explain the difference between being sorry and being guilty. Love and honesty are your best weapons.

Anxiety

This is created by self-doubt, unhappiness and insecurity. When a child feels unsafe in any way, this feeling forms the first building block of anxiety. The more loved and approved of really used when you walk in, eat a meal and then walk out without thanking me' rather than 'You're so selfish. You never thank me for cooking. I'm sick of you', which is an attack on the other person. When we exhibit negative anger, we always go on the attack; when we practise the expression of positive anger, we can bring about change without abuse and nastiness.

Jealousy

For as long as you can remember, you have probably been dealing with jealousy in your children. When they were small, it was over things like toys, outings, attention and praise. As teenagers, they are less likely to tell you what they're jealous about but it will probably relate to friends, grades, looks and money. If they do talk to you, you can advise them about the futility of the green-eyed monster, tell them that they are special, with many gifts, and need not envy anyone. But it's your actions that will speak louder than your words. If they see you displaying jealous feelings over your friends or neighbours, they will follow suit.

It's also very important that you don't scoff at their feelings as they appear. Don't trivialise petty jealousies as they are probably very real to your child. Try not to say things like 'That's not worth worrying about' or 'What do you see in that girl, anyway?'

Give your teenager lots of praise, especially credit for improvement. That's one of the most common complaints I hear from teenagers against their parents: 'No matter how hard I try, they don't even notice my efforts. They never tell me I'm doing well.'

Guilt

It's not necessary to have something to feel guilty about. It's part and parcel of the human experience. Unfortunately, I have to say that most guilt is instilled in childhood, in homes and

40 ■ TEENAGE STRESS

and, on the whole, frown on excessive demonstration of feelings, unlike, for example, southern Europeans who show what they feel — grief, joy, anger — without restraint. I remember being amazed on a trip to Greece when perfect strangers would start screaming at each other in a public place over something as trivial as a spilt drink or a 'stolen' seat. Maybe we don't wish to go to those extremes but we could be a little freer and less inhibited about our feelings. Certainly, I think we can all be more generous with our praise, shows of affection, our smiles and laughter. Laughter is one of the most therapeutic things available to us and it's free! You may not feel like laughing at some of the antics of your teenagers but a sense of humour can go a long way towards defusing the tension in a situation.

So, here are some tips on dealing with anger.

■ Remember anger is not always expressed immediately, so look beyond the current situation to find clues.

■ The old idea of counting to ten does work, simply because anger often evaporates as quickly as it rises and the time delay gives you a chance to 'cool down'.

■ It's always better to wait till you're no longer angry before thrashing out ongoing problems.

■ Learn to distinguish between the trivial anger events and those that mask deeper problems which ought to be talked out later.

■ When your child is very angry towards you, try not to retaliate. For instance, saying to your teenagers, 'How dare you speak to me like that' is meaningless because they've already done it. It's much better to look past your own ego and pride, see their pain and try to understand why they're angry.

■ It's always better to express anger in a calm rational way, as it happens. Anger is not always loud and forceful, it can be internal and cold. If you repress it, it will come out at a later date in a far more negative way.

■ Own up to your feelings and accept responsibility for them by using 'I' when describing them. For example, say 'I feel

EMOTIONS ■ 39

disagree with their decisions. At the same time, you need to set distinct boundaries so that, while they're experimenting with life, they can still feel safe.

In the area of emotions, the key word is confusion. Life is a mass of contradictions for all of us, but so much more so for the teenager who lives in a twilight world between adulthood and childhood, adult feelings and childish needs. They have a desire for freedom and taking risks, but they are full of terror and uncertainty. No matter how badly they seem to behave at times, can we have anything but compassion for them? Of course, some will play on your emotions and milk them to their own ends. That just comes with the territory, and I'm sure that with experience, you can learn to resist their emotional blackmail.

It might help if you understood the nature of the negative emotions that plague your teenagers. There is scope here to look only at the key emotions.

Anger

Anger is rarely related to the event of the moment. It's much more likely to be about a quarrel you had two weeks ago or a stored resentment. So when you say to your teenager, 'Your room looks a bit messy', you may only be teasing and are amazed at the violent response you get, such as a volley of swearing or a yelling fit. It's quite possible that your son or daughter has just had a run-in with a teacher, has just discovered a new pimple, or hasn't got a date for the dance next weekend. In other words, it's not about you at all, but you happened to be there and copped it. A wise parent lets this sort of behaviour pass — but what if you've had a bad day yourself, or if you're unemployed and worried about money, or if you're going through a mid-life crisis? You also need to recognise these factors in yourself and practise anger management.

None of us, at any age, finds it easy to deal with strong emotion. Australians are not known for their emotional natures

5 Emotions

I don't need to tell you that your teenagers are emotional! That has been the key message of the book so far — that most teenage stress is emotional. You live with this fact every day if you have a teenager in your house. Unfortunately, because of the extreme changes your teenagers are going through, they will be experiencing negative emotions such as anger, jealousy, guilt and anxiety far more than the positive emotions of love, compassion, kindness, joy.

All emotions are valid, and are simply part of the wide spectrum of experience that comprises human life. That's something you, as parents, can easily lose sight of in your desire to teach your children the 'right' things. When they were small, you spent a lot of time correcting their 'bad' behaviours, curbing their temper tantrums, giving them instructions about morality and so on. This is part of your responsibility as parents, but now that you have teenagers, it probably seems they've forgotten all you said. They defy the rules, exhibit bad manners, seem to care about no one but themselves, and speak rudely if you say anything. Do you give up and let them go for it or do you battle on, even if it creates continual conflict? The $64,000 question!

I have already said in chapter 2 that compromise is the answer. It's best to give sufficient rope so that your teenagers can exercise some freedom of choice even if you strongly

SEXUALITY ■ 37

is eternally inflammatory, as it exposes one of the most vulnerable areas of human existence. Counsellors like me treat the scarred and wounded people who grapple with feelings of sexual inadequacy, the frustration of dysfunction and the fears of intimacy and relationships. These problems are planted in childhood and take root in the teenage years. How you as parents handle the training of your children can make all the difference.

36 ■ TEENAGE STRESS

a double life, sometimes well past teenage. If you put yourself in your child's shoes, you wouldn't want to put them through this torture, I'm sure. You cannot make your children exist off a perfect blueprint that you made for them, and this applies whether it's to do with their sexual behaviour, their values in life, the friends they choose or the life-choices they make. Your decision, therefore, has to be whether you want to keep them near in love and acceptance or try to force them into your mould and push them away. The only question you have to ask yourself is: is my child more important than my pride?

If you cannot approve of your gay daughter or son, still love, learn to accept, and offer unconditional support. As with all other teenage problems, there is no easy answer — just more love, tolerance and knowledge.

Sexual activity

What if your teenager tells you he/she is ready to go ahead and have sex? After you gently listen, counsel on the pitfalls and speak your objections, what should you do next?

- Advise on contraception. Find out what your teenager already knows and go from there.
- Ensure that they understand the physical, health and emotional implications.
- Make an appointment for your daughter or son to see a GP, a counsellor or a minister.
- Ask some relevant questions about location and plan for the first sexual encounter, as most people have unpleasant memories of early fumblings and abortive attempts at having sex.

Once you've done all this, you cannot do any more. Trust the teenager you raised to make the right decision even if you don't agree with it.

This chapter has probably raised as many questions as it has supplied answers, and is likely to be the most controversial discussion of any in the book. Sex, as a subject in our society,

SEXUALITY ■ 35

behaviours, stem from insensitive handling of teenagers and children. Masturbation should be just one of a number of normal topics covered in your discussions about sex with your teenager. If you feel that it's excessive or in any other way problematic, you could talk to your teenager about it specifically, but otherwise, it will take its natural course without your intervention. If you have strong religious or moral objections, I suggest you talk to your child about your feelings before it becomes an issue. Guilt instilled in childhood can never be erased and can play an obstructive role to normal sexual development.

Homosexuality

Your children are sex-typed very early in life, and, in most cases, they conform to your gender expectations. However, in some cases, you may have a little girl who wants to act the tomboy or a boy who dresses up and likes to use lipstick. This can be another form of normal experimentation, or it can be a signpost to your child's future sexuality. No-one has an absolute answer to the question, why is approximately 10 per cent of any population homosexual? If your teenager falls into this section of society, your response is going to be crucial. How are you going to react when your teenager comes to you and announces, 'I think I'm gay'? Very few of you can be expected to react positively or even neutrally as this is such an emotional issue in Australian society.

I can't tell you how you should feel or what you ought to do, but let me say this: this would have to be one of the most difficult admissions your teenager will ever have to make, and it must take tremendous courage. If you then jump up and down, ridicule, scold or reject, immediately you will alienate your child. Many of them will never tell you about their sexual preferences, preferring to 'stay in the closet' until they leave home. Yet others live in abject fear and guilt of being caught, some deny their feelings out of shame, and still others live

34 ■ TEENAGE STRESS

today, and you as parents have a voice in this. Don't let your children be shielded from the less pleasant aspects of life because life itself won't shield them; you're not doing them any favours by dealing in half-truths or taking the attitude that 'they'll find out soon enough'.

The challenge for educators is to harness all that youthful energy and enthusiasm while teaching the values of commitment and discipline. The key lies in building relationships that are based on honesty and open communication. As children grow into teenagers, you can easily become the enemy, almost irrelevant bystanders, and the more you push and pressure, the more you promote an emotional stalemate. Wise parents slacken the leash sufficiently to allow freedom of choice within boundaries of love and patience.

Masturbation

One of the most destructive things you can do as a parent is to ridicule or scold your child when you catch him/her masturbating. I say 'when' rather than 'if' because they are rare teenagers indeed who do not at some time during puberty and the ensuing years touch themselves in a sexually exploratory way. As this activity is most likely to occur at home, you may come across your teenager masturbating at any time, or at least have an awareness that it's going on. The best action to take is none, as this is a perfectly natural stage of growth and no focus of attention should be placed on it.

Most teenagers are past the bed-wetting stage, but I knew of one girl who suffered incontinence day and night due to a bladder condition. The shame was much worse than the physical problem for this girl, and it required a deft touch on the part of her mother, in particular, as a negative response would have damaged the girl emotionally. The same applies in the case of masturbating. Many sexual problems that manifest in later life such as impotence, premature ejaculation, voyeurism, exposing genitalia in public and other deviant

SEXUALITY ■ 33

talk to sons about sex and mothers to talk to daughters. It stands to reason that a woman can understand what's going on in her daughter's body far better, and a man his son's. In one-parent families it can sometimes be a bit awkward, as in the case of the father who did not know how to instruct his daughter in the use of sanitary pads, but usually a suitable relative can fill in.

Sex education in the home is not just about giving out information. Attitudes too are taught via body language, speech, actions and behaviour. If a teenager lives in a home where no affection is ever shown, that will be accepted as the norm and as the role-model for future married life. Sex is an activity that, in the main, takes place in the home and that's why I strongly advocate that it is positively taught in the home. I'm sure you would rather they learn from you than from 'dirty' books or ill-informed peers.

Supplementary sex education at school is also vital, and if your teenagers are not enrolled in a programme, see the principal and look into the possibility of visiting experts. You need a forum for discussion under adult supervision. I remember a few years ago, when I was teaching English in a country town, a fuss being made about a particular text that was on the Year 11 curriculum. The main objection was the bad language and frankness in regard to love-making. My argument was that the students know these swear words anyway, and isn't it better that they hear them in class in the right context so that they can be instructed that there's a time and place for strong language? Also, literature is supposed to address human issues. What kind of false education are we giving our students if we don't talk about sex and love openly? Isn't it better that they have a caring, sensitive teacher to canvass their options with rather than read these books (which they undoubtedly will, anyway) in isolation where they might miss the point of the story? School is surely not only a place for learning about history, maths and grammar. What about equipping our young people for life outside the classroom? Censorship of targeted books still does occur in our schools

32 ■ TEENAGE STRESS

go along. For example, give names to genitalia — penis, vagina, nipple, etc — if you are seen in the shower or walking around in the nude in your bedroom. Small children are bound to ask questions, especially if there's no brother or sister to compare with. A little boy is quite likely to ask his mother why she hasn't got a 'willy'. Here's a perfect opportunity to explain that Mums and Dads are different, and that his willy is really a 'penis' and Mummy has a vagina. A toddler will accept this quite naturally as long as it's not overdone or forced.

Another very desirable method is to answer your children's questions as frankly as possible, as they come up. Children have a natural curiosity and would rather be told when they want to know than when parents decide to instruct. The amount and style of information you offer will depend on the sex and age-group you're dealing with. Obviously, you wouldn't talk in the same way to a seven-year-old boy as you would to a seventeen-year-old girl. As they get older, they will develop a tendency to be more secretive and introspective, especially in personal matters. Thus, as puberty begins, and they need information and guidance more, the communication gap between parents and child grows wider — this is one of the many contradictions that beset teenagers and their bewildered parents.

If you are reluctant to talk to your children about sex, it could be for a number of reasons. Perhaps you grew up in a household where sex was a taboo subject, or you feel inadequate to the task, or you just feel too embarrassed to even start. Most of you fall into the middle category. You offer minimal information and hope they'll find out the rest elsewhere. From my counselling experience, far more teenagers find out about sex 'along the way' than is healthy or desirable.

Yet, it's better for you to say nothing at all than to put negative concepts and ideas into young, impressionable minds, such as mothers telling daughters that men 'only want one thing', or fathers talking about women as if they are nothing more than bed partners. It is generally considered better for fathers to

SEXUALITY ■ 31

smorgasbord these days. With the best will in the world, and short of keeping your children chained up in the basement, you will not be able to prevent them putting themselves to the test in many emotional and physical arenas. Hopefully, if you are willing to address issues honestly, your teenagers will come to you for guidance.

The AIDS Council exists partly to disseminate information about the disease and, in particular, prevention of risk. You can get pamphlets and attend seminars to educate yourself on this widespread problem. The Family Planning Association of Australia has an educational arm that offers phone advice, workshops and qualified counsellors to help young people in matters of contraception, health and sexual attitudes. The major churches also offer counselling and educational programmes, and some of you may prefer your children to learn about sex and growing up within the context of your family religion.

Sex education

Early sex education at home and at school is the best start you can give your children. Some of you may not be comfortable with your own sexuality and are therefore embarrassed about speaking openly with your teenagers. You may be reluctant or unable to play a teaching role in this area. There are excellent books available which introduce young people to the biological facts and emotional considerations of human sexuality. Ideally, these are used in conjunction with parental and school guidance rather than as a replacement.

The more natural the method of sex education, the more effective. There's no point in sitting a thirteen-year old down and announcing that you're going to tell them about sex! For a start, they're likely to already know some of the rudiments, and they'll be so embarrassed, they won't benefit from anything you tell them. It's best if information is offered at the child's pace. If you feel at home with your own bodies, with nudity and sexuality, it's probably best to teach your children as you

4 Sexuality

You probably worry more about your teenagers' sexual development than any other single factor in their growth, for the simple reason that there appear to be more pitfalls and hazards in this part of their lives. Let's examine in detail each of your main concerns.

Health education

If your teenagers are going to experiment with sex, are they minimising the risks and looking after themselves? The best way for you to ensure that they do is to arm them with as much knowledge as you personally can, and then, point them in the direction they need to find out the rest. Answer their questions as honestly as you can when they're growing up and keep the lines of communication open as they enter young adulthood in their teen years.

The argument that if teenagers are told too much, it'll just encourage them to go out and try things for themselves doesn't wash in the 90s. Knowledge is power and enables young people to make enlightened choices. Preventing AIDS is not the only reason to refuse sex or use condoms. Teenagers are natural experimenters and they will want to try things no matter how much we as adults advise them not to. Life is one huge

SCHOOL ■ 29

being diagnosed as dyslexic, which is a learning disorder that can be corrected. Sometimes, it's poor eyesight or the seating arrangements in class or a personality conflict with a particular teacher. Get to the root of the problem before scolding and criticising. Even if it turns out to be just laziness or poor work habits, a positive game plan can turn the situation around. My whole approach to problems of any kind is that knowledge is always the first step. You can't improve anything if you don't know what's wrong or what you want to change.

In chapter 2, we saw the importance of home life to the teenager who is often unhappy and confused. The majority of teenagers attend school or college so learning, exams, the demands of teachers, the pressure of deadlines, social and personal relationships are part and parcel of the luggage in the average teenager's life. The bottom line is that home life can either be a comfort or another battleground to conquer. There are no pat answers or quick fixes, unfortunately. You and your teenager have to work through it day by day, struggle by struggle, in love and anger, in success and failure.

28 ■ TEENAGE STRESS

at these crucial junctures. Unfortunately, many parents and teachers forget what it was like to be six, twelve and seventeen. It's an old saying that we 'can't put an old head on young shoulders'. Making mistakes and doing 'stupid' things is part of growing up. A sense of humour is an invaluable tool, although I am told by parents of teenagers that they fast lose theirs after the first couple of hundred crises. Just grin and bear it. It only lasts for six years!

■ If your teenager lives away from home for any reason, for example, attends boarding-school, he/she is removed from your daily supervision and, therefore, a lot of what I've said will not apply. However, the transition involved in leaving home and becoming a boarder at a school is a very difficult adjustment for both child and parent, especially when the child is very young. Some kids go as early as Grade 4 or 5. Your continued support and interest are essential. You haven't handed over your children to another authority to take your place. Your role as parent is unique and can never be usurped. I taught many boarders during my time in high schools and saw first-hand the loneliness and isolation of young people who were dreadfully homesick and felt alienated in their new environment. Knowing you care and take the trouble to keep in close contact via letters, phone calls and visits can make all the difference.

Learning difficulties

A tutor can be useful in certain cases as a short-term measure. If you have expertise in a particular area, such as maths or English, or if you are a teacher yourself, you can be a source of comfort and clarity for your children. The most important ingredient in this interaction is patience, as you are unlikely to be consulted if you ridicule or lose your temper.

Trace the origins of any particular learning difficulty your teenager has, if possible, as treatment may be available. For example, a lot of poor spellers and writers at school end up and take the job (which would only be a stopgap until marriage) or stick it out another year and risk unemployment at the end of the road. My advice was to examine her own priorities and decide her long-term goals as they would give her a clear path to follow.

So many teenagers feel pressured by their parents' desires and goals for their future. In families where there's a long tradition in a certain trade or profession, there might even exist a foregone conclusion that the teenager will go into law or medicine or plumbing, whatever it might be. Today's competitiveness in regard to school achievements and job opportunities can cause parents to be over-anxious and aggressively demanding.

The higher the family is on the socio-economic scale, the worse the problem seems to be. In extreme cases, teenagers can be hounded to perform at a certain level, such as with the boy in the recent film *Dead Poet's Society.* It's a fine line between being vigilant over your teenager's progress and being obsessive, a line that you have to monitor constantly in order to avoid crossing it. It's important that you ask, listen, guide, offer and suggest rather than tell. Your teenagers want your approval — never doubt that — and they may make incorrect decisions for themselves in an effort to please you. A simple way to avoid this is to always open up instead of closing off or narrowing down. Canvass all the options available and let the solution come naturally.

Transitions

Your children make three very important transitions during their school life: starting school, moving from primary school to high school, and leaving school. These are, therefore, the most stressful periods and, from my experience as a counsellor, the times at which kids are most prone to emotional breakdown and at which their relationships are most strained. Just knowing this should help you to be more patient with your children

26 ■ TEENAGE STRESS

to blame for your teenagers' apathy, but the way you treat them can make a big difference. Even the simple acts of listening, asking interested (but not prying) questions, making time for them, can spell the difference between success and failure, joy and misery. I personally don't agree with parents 'buying' good grades and good behaviour with gifts, but this is a very individual choice. If it works in your family and the gifts are given in the right spirit, there's no reason it can't be an aid to the whole process. But if teenagers work hard just to get a new TV or CD player, I see little long-term benefit.

■ *Monitor balance.* If you see your teenagers overdoing one aspect of their lives, such as school work or social activities, counselling them to rethink their priorities might be helpful. As I said in the last chapter, your advice is unlikely to be popular or heeded but if it's offered without pressure, change might subtly evolve. One of the hardest things to do is make a suggestion and then walk away without resolution, particularly for parents who tend to want to press the point until it's accepted. The teenager feels cornered and instead of a useful exchange, the incident develops into a battle of wills.

I remember a parent phoning me when I was teaching a human relations course to a Year 10 class. She thanked me for talking to her daughter about such issues as dating, pre-marital sex, smoking and alcohol because, as she put it, 'I *am* here for my daughter. She could talk to me openly but she won't because I'm her mother. So, I'm glad you're there for her to discuss these matters with.'

Always keep the lines of communication open whether the option is taken up or not. It's a vital safety net for your teenage children.

■ *Respect future goals.* A Year 11 student came to talk to me once about a crossroads she found herself at. A bright student, she had the ability to go on to tertiary studies but she was Italian and had had an offer of a job in the family business. Her choice: to leave school at the end of Year 11

SCHOOL ▪ 25

would come home when she was working at the kitchen table and rail at her because he was drunk. On some occasions, he would sweep all her books, notes and pads off the table and chase her out of the room. Such obstacles to learning are not as isolated as we might imagine. Others range from noise to quarrelling, from ridicule to pressure such as 'How long will you be with that homework? I need to lay the table for breakfast.' You can't do your teenagers' work for them but you do owe them support and help.

▪ *Learning doesn't only come in formal packages.* Ask yourself these questions: Do you encourage your children to discuss their ideas, concerns, projects with you? Do you as a family talk about a variety of topics or do you just watch TV over dinner or have loud music blasting endlessly so that quiet contemplation and sharing is impossible? Is there a reasonable library of books, tapes, videos and other resources in your home? Are your children encouraged in their natural curiosity for knowledge or do you shush them if they speak to you at an inopportune moment? Studies prove that the best achievers come from homes where learning and achievement are respected values.

▪ *Offer incentives.* Some kids insist they work better in front of TV or with the radio blasting. I'd be a bit sceptical, but I don't believe in deprivation as a form of discipline. I'm sure that positive reinforcement works better. Give your teenager responsibility over his/her own choices and only take away privileges if your trust is abused. Praise lavishly if grades improve and encourage enthusiasm for schoolwork, because motivation is a vital key to learning. Whatever praise you give will be absorbed like a sponge soaking up water, although it may not be made evident on the spot.

The same applies to criticism. I can't emphasise enough the importance of helping your teenagers feel good about themselves. One of the most common complaints from teenagers about their parents is that they feel that whatever they do is never good enough. Eventually, the attitude becomes, 'Why should I bother to keep trying?' You are not

24 ■ TEENAGE STRESS

foreign to you. Some parents insist on helping even when they know nothing about the subject matter or method required, especially in an area like maths which has undergone enormous changes in the last decade.

This only makes schoolwork more difficult for your child as he/she not only has the original problem but now has to risk offending you by refusing your unwelcome help.

How then to be of real help?

■ *Wait to be asked.* It's not helpful to insist on showing 'how good I was in science when I was at school'. This attitude can end up wasting your child's precious homework time and even jeopardise the ultimate success of the work. If you are asked and don't know the answer, either suggest a source of information that your child can consult or work through the material together, making it clear that you don't have the necessary knowledge. That's the principle I adopted in the classroom. I never pretended to know the answer to a student's question if I didn't, as it gave us an opportunity to find out together. Learning becomes an adventure that way. At the same time, guide but don't do the work for your teenagers. No matter how well-meaning your motives, you'll actually be doing more harm than good.

■ *Provide a pleasant learning environment.* This is essential. As a teacher, I soon learnt not to prejudge the reasons for my student's actions. For instance, in the case of homework, a child who consistently fails to hand in their assignments may not simply be lazy. Very often, their homes are not conducive to quiet study. If you can possibly afford the space and cost, give your child a desk in the bedroom. Doing homework at the kitchen table is not a satisfactory alternative but it's often all that's available. If that's the case at your place, let it be quiet at least and allow the student to work uninterrupted. A dining table or desk in a separate room would still be preferable.

In one extreme case, I found out some months after the problem began that the reason for a student's chronic neglect of homework was an alcoholic father. Every evening, he

3 School

Despite the fact that you're not physically present at school with your children, your influence goes with them and they bring home the stresses they live with in the classroom and playground, so read on. You have a vital part to play.

When you handed your children over on their first day at school, you relinquished a large part of your influence over them. But, as we saw in chapter 2, what happens at home affects young people in an ongoing way all through their school life and into adulthood. As society becomes more and more complicated, children find school ever more stressful, and a harmonious home life is vital.

When they reach their teenage years, it's as if all the demands and pressures of juggling home, personal and school commitments close in on them, and that's why teenagers often appear to be distracted or 'on the edge'. The very thing they crave is the very thing they seem to reject. You have your work cut out for you just to keep things at home on an even keel. But there are specific ways in which you can directly reduce stress for your teenage child at school.

Homework

A lot of the work your teenager brings home will be totally

23

22 ■ TEENAGE STRESS

to sleep every single night. I felt abandoned and desolate. To this day, I still have a hangup about being 'left', even though, in reality, my important relationships have all been long-lasting. I only came to understand this recently. I tell this story as an illustration of the effect of childhood experiences on adult life.

What children of all ages need more than anything is security. It's more vital than the type of food they eat, the clothing they wear, the house they live in, the toys they play with, or any other single thing. They may not show their appreciation of you but look for the subtle signs of love. They're there if you want to see them.

I received this letter from a teenager a few years ago and I think it sums up very well the lost confusion of this age-group:

'I'm trapped on a lonely stage and I'm the only actor. I've lost complete sense of reality. I'm seventeen years old and I've been day-dreaming ever since I was seven. I left school last year and have since been stuck at home. I have erased memories and built up expectations and strange identities. I can't sleep at night and sometimes wake up the household with my banging, talking and running around. I'm scared to get help because I don't know what I'm going to do when I come out of my problem. I don't even know if I want a job. I have no close friends and I'm not close to my family. I'm still a child and I don't ever want to grow up. Most of the time I think of suicide because I feel like a nobody, that I have nothing to offer this world but I do want to live in reality. My family don't understand me and I don't understand myself. I hate being an island. Please help me.'

YOUR HOME ■ 21

door is a slaughterhouse.' If this is true, what a sad indictment of our society. If there is any place that we should always feel safe to go to, it's our own home; yet how many teenagers dread going home each day to interrogation, criticism, scrutiny, rebuke or, worst of all, indifference? Families need to support and love each other, and while every individual member has a part to play, you as the parents have the added burden of responsibility; you are the family caretakers. Let your teenagers find their own way but never forget that they need you despite their bravado and tough exteriors.

Perhaps the best advice I can leave you with is: don't expect to win. If you're too kind and soft, you'll be accused of not caring enough, if you're strict, you'll be accused of not caring at all, and even if you're the very best parents in the world, your teenager may appear to be fonder of the cat or a neighbour or an uncle. This whole issue is not about justice but about what *is*. After all, acceptance is perhaps one of the most vital components of love.

I loved and adored my mother but her biggest crime in my eyes was that she was too young-looking. I used to long for an old, grey-haired Mum who knitted and baked cookies, instead of an attractive, vital, middle-aged woman with five times more zip than I had! My friends all envied me a mother who treated me more like a sister and friend than a daughter, but I would gladly have swapped for one of their nagging, fussing mothers because I equated those behaviours with love. My mother never told me to wear my raincoat, she liked all my boyfriends and she was happy to talk to me about any subject. As a teenager, I was not grateful for what I had but wanted to shape a parent out of my own needs and desires. Now, of course, I can look back and view the situation quite differently. Ah, the wisdom of hindsight!

When I was about eight years old, my mother went on an extended overseas trip and put me into a boarding school for three terms. I had other family members to keep an eye on me and Mum wrote every week, but I loathed and detested being away from her and my home. I remember crying myself

20 ■ TEENAGE STRESS

have done the best job possible as a parent then trust the child you raised and accept the problems your teenager brings home, accept the pain they may inflict on themselves, on you and on the family in general, and accept the joys and the disappointments. But if you know yourself to be guilty of neglect or cruelty or any other unloving behaviour, try to make up for it by being there now. It's never too late, and the requirements are relatively simple.

Let your home be a haven for your teenagers, not a place of conflict and anger. Let them bring friends home. Be more concerned about their happiness than their grades, appearance, the state of your house. Let love guide you to the right priorities and, when you fail, forgive yourself first so that you can forgive your kids and not vent your frustrations and impatience on them. Practise 'tough love', that is, be firm when it's necessary, even if it makes you unpopular. Giving in to your kids is easy but teaches them nothing and being overly-rigid breeds resentment, so you need to find a middle road.

It sounds rather like sainthood, doesn't it, but it doesn't have to be that one-sided. By giving yourself at this crucial time in your child's life, you will be immensely rewarded. The home is the foundation for the adult person. Most of our most painful and joyful experiences take place during childhood in the home. In any average home at any given time, there can be up to four generations going through a variety of personal crises yet somehow having to deal with each other. Teenagers have to cope with their own considerable conflicts while around them emotional problems to do with such things as money, sex, love, communication and work are raging.

Parents, you have the most awesome responsibility and the most important job in the world. And because you are human, you will fail at it as often as you succeed. For this your children may never forgive you, because they want the perfect parents they believed you to be when they were small. But if you concentrate on having a real relationship with your children, they will come back to you after the dark days of the teenage years are over. Laurence Olivier once said, 'Behind every front

YOUR HOME ■ 19

and teach them the important values that never change. Try to speak their language, even though this will no doubt be very difficult for you. Talk about things that interest them, indulge their tastes in music, clothes and films, and, where you disagree, find a middle ground.

Kahlil Gibran, the Lebanese poet, expressed these feelings beautifully in the following poem:

And a woman who held a babe against her bosom said, Speak to us of Children.
And he said:
Your children are not your children.
They are the sons and daughters of Life's longing for itself.
They come through you but not from you,
And though they are with you yet they belong not to you.
You may give them your love but not your thoughts,
For they have their own thoughts.
You may house their bodies but not their souls,
For their souls dwell in the house of to-morrow,
which you cannot visit, not even in your dreams.
You may strive to be like them, but seek not to make them like you.
For life goes not backward nor tarries with yesterday.
You are the bows from which your children as living arrows are sent forth.

Whatever your teenagers are doing in their lives comes straight back to land on your front door. So if they're vandalising, stealing, taking drugs, dropping out of school or getting drunk, society is going to blame you, just as you would expect to take the credit if they turn out to be star athletes or scholars or simply good human beings. If you believe you

18 ■ TEENAGE STRESS

enough to love your children when they were small, helpless and seemed to need you so much. Your teenager, on the other hand, is arrogant, argumentative and totally unlovable. What you might be missing is the vulnerability they can't show but feel deeply. They are terrified most of the time and unable to talk about it. They need your compassion and understanding just as much as they ever did. Now is the time to test the real depth of your love, now when your children are hard to love, when they're painful to be around, when they're no longer the little darlings that relatives can coo over, but rather unwashed horrors you'd rather disown.

Even if your particular teenagers don't fit into this category, it's quite likely that they do things that bug you or frighten you or threaten you. Love them unconditionally. This is the most fragile time you're ever going to have with your children. Rifts formed now can be permanent, and many teenagers leave home never to return. I'm not suggesting you give in to them in order to keep them. In fact, teenagers need and value discipline, as long as it is dished out with equal amounts of love and is fairly administered. Teenagers don't reject parents because they're strict but because they are unloving, don't give them time and attention, put them down, are inflexible with rules, play power games and treat them with a lack of respect for their individuality.

Your children don't belong to you; they never did, but perhaps you didn't know it until they became teenagers and now, suddenly, you're having to deal with that fact. You brought them into this world and so you owe them food, shelter and care. For those things, you can demand respect and love but you're unlikely to get them by saying things like 'I have a right to choose your friends because I gave you life!' or 'How can you speak to me like that after all I've done for you!'

The way you did things when you were their age is not relevant; your children live in a different world. Harping on about how you used to think, act and behave will only drive a bigger wedge between you. All you can do is guide them whether it's a relatively trivial matter such as how long to have their hair or as important as where they go to study or work. Children lack power in our society but generally don't rebel except in extreme cases. Teenagers rebel as a matter of course. Even if you are the most reasonable and understanding parent, you will no doubt be criticised and rejected. Fairness has nothing to do with it. Keep in mind that your teenager is a tyrant and quite likely to be the one in control, instead of you. They will not hesitate to manipulate people and situations if it means getting what they want. Therefore, your home can easily become a battleground if the everyday tensions aren't diffused.

The family meeting is a way for members to have their say and for problems to be thrashed out in an orderly and frank manner. Such issues as use of household facilities, curfews and chores can be discussed, as well as more personal subjects. If you decide to try this strategy, don't be surprised if you are met with total silence at first. Mums are usually all for it, Dads have to be convinced it's not all a waste of time, and kids often resent the whole exercise. It takes a lot of time to build up the sort of trust required for these sessions to work, but I have seen tremendous results from them when they're done properly.

Some families even write up a contract based on the agreements arrived at in the conference situation. This is up to you. Trial and error is your best bet: whatever works for your family is the best medicine. I'm also a great advocate of the old theory that prevention is better than cure. Many human problems are allowed to continue until they take on much larger proportions than they need to. If we have enough information and enough love, we can solve many of our own problems and prevent others developing.

Love

As simplistic as it might sound, what your teenager needs more than anything from you is love. You probably found it easy

16 ■ TEENAGE STRESS

he did, his brother had been there before. He was so sick of hearing about his brother's abilities and achievements, but felt powerless to change the situation. When I asked him about his rages, he said he could never remember losing his temper; it was almost like a blackout. My suggestion to him was to find a particular interest and hobby that was his alone and excel at it. Luckily, he already had one, surfing, something his brother didn't do. That was a start, but it took a lot of therapy to help him work through his frustration and anger at simply being the second to be born.

Jane. Brad's counterpart, except a different gender. Again, Jane was the second child, this time with an older sister. Her case was complicated by her sister and her mother both being great beauties with poise and grace, while Jane was lumpy, plain and awkward. She was in a class I taught for a time and I rarely saw a more unhappy child. Her misery manifested itself in bad behaviour, rebellion and a 'smart mouth'.

Gwen. Gwen was a second child with an older sister and a number of other siblings. I met her at a boarding school where I was teaching. Again, she was a plain, uncomfortable child languishing in the shadow of a pretty sister's popularity and unquestioned superiority. Their mother would come to visit the school and see only the older sister, leaving Gwen devastated and feeling very much second-best. She too was always in trouble in class and unpopular with teachers and fellow-students — but one has to wonder how much of this behaviour was predisposed by the lack of expectation on everyone's part for a second child to shine.

The family conference

One of the best things you can do as a family group is to hold regular conferences. In the same way as business people convene to discuss strategies, productivity and problems, families can iron out their differences in this very positive way. It certainly beats yelling, fighting or sulking. Teenagers want to feel empowered within their own framework of life-choices,

YOUR HOME ■ 15

However, there's also a lot more expected of the eldest child, especially after the others arrive. Parents tend to say things like 'You have to set a good example for your younger brothers and sisters' or 'Be Mummy's good little helper'. This type of message creates a 'goody-goody' child who will generally do as ordered, is dutiful and respectful but also rather too disciplined. Remember, you make all your worst parenting mistakes with your first child.

By the time the second child comes, the glow is a little less bright, the novelty has worn off. So the demands and expectations are less, but so is the feeling of being special. Second children, also known as 'sandwich' children if they are between numbers one and three, have been the focus of the most intense research because they often have the hardest time of it. They live forever in the shadow of their 'perfect' older sibling, feel inferior, have a lot less attention paid to them, and are generally insecure and more nervous.

If there is a third child, he/she has the easiest time because by now parents are getting pretty good at this 'bringing up kids' thing, they're older and wiser, usually more financially secure, and feel less need to spend time in the house keeping watch. Which all means that the youngest member of the household can get away with a lot more. If the child was unplanned, he/she is often regarded as a special gift and fussed over in a way not seen with earlier arrivals.

An only child is pretty much the same as the first in a psychological sense but will be characterised by a tendency towards solitary pastimes, will be very independent and used to spending a lot of time alone, for obvious reasons.

When dealing with your teenager, keep these descriptions in mind as they might offer a lot of insight into your child's behaviour and the way you interact with him/her. Here are three case samples that will reinforce the impact of this positioning.

Brad. His parents brought him in for counselling with me because of his uncontrollable fits of rage. He was the second son in a family of two and he told me that no matter what

14 ■ TEENAGE STRESS

all the time, but children, especially teenagers, want honesty. If you know you've been unfair, apologise and move on. It amazes me how many parents think it's somehow humiliating to admit they're wrong to their children, and refuse to do it even when they know they should. I once asked a class of teenagers to write down the qualities they most liked in adults. The three winning qualities were fairness, sense of humour and honesty, in that order.

So, what are some of the best strategies to employ when dealing with your teenagers?

- Keep rules clear, simple and to a minimum.
- Keep lines of communication open at all times.
- Let your kids know that you are human. Don't try to be 'superparents'.
- Put limits on your giving. Giving all the time isn't necessarily love.
- Try to be positive even when you have to chastise.
- Be as consistent as possible, especially with rules.
- Let your children see that you have needs as well.
- Use as little physical discipline as possible. I know you only strike out in frustration, but it really isn't the answer to any problem that may face your family. A little hitting goes a long way.
- Respect your teenagers' privacy. Let them have their rooms the way they want them. Knock before you go in. Don't snoop around when they're out.

Good parenting skills are learned, not God-given. You tend to cut your teeth on your first child, take your second one for granted, and spoil your third and subsequent children. This has been determined by research into the significance of position in a family. Let me give you some more details and you can decide how it relates to your family unit.

First, second or subsequent child?

The first child in a family is doted on and always feels special.

YOUR HOME ■ 13

the mother can trust the way she has brought this boy up, the values she's instilled in him, she can rest in the knowledge that he will come back to the child she knows despite his growing and changing.

Problem: Staying out. Parents have to adjust to their teenage son suddenly staying out all night without warning, and even not turning up home for several days. The boy has always been exceptionally dependable and considerate. The first time he stayed out, the mother rang every hospital in the area and worried herself sick. When he showed up, she let him have it with both barrels. He couldn't see what the fuss was about. What can parents do in these situations?

Solution: The mother probably did overreact but it was understandable in the circumstances. The problem was worsened by the fact that the behaviour was not characteristic of her son, therefore unexpected. When the dust settled, it should be explained to the boy that he did a thoughtless thing, that it wasn't just the staying out which was the problem but the lack of communication. Ground rules could then be set by mutual agreement and a compromise set for the future.

Problem: Large families. A mother with eight children expressed concern to me at a seminar in regard to her interaction with each child. 'How can I give myself equally to each of my children when I'm run ragged just keeping up with all I have to do?' A very reasonable question!

Solution: The answer lies in compromise and in letting children know that you're human. For instance, if one particular child needs help with homework and you're busy bathing another, it's hurtful to simply reject the request for help with an 'I'm too busy, love'. Children in large families often speak of feeling lost in the shuffle, of suffering from a lack of identity and not getting enough attention. You need to be sensitive to this and make each child feel as special as possible. Loving communication is a good tool. In this case, a quiet explanation that Mum is occupied right now and can only do one thing effectively at a time **but** is happy to help in a few moments.

Obviously, no parent is going to be patient and reasonable

12 ■ TEENAGE STRESS

but as society diversifies more and more this pattern, known as the 'nuclear family', is altered and modified. Quite commonly there is only a single parent, sometimes only one child or, less often, a huge family of children, six or more; 'parents' can be two homosexuals or two friends who share a house, or any other combination of adults. European families sometimes have three or more generations living under one roof.

Each of these styles of living brings resultant stresses, but the scope of this book does not allow for examination of each individually. Suffice it to say that, obviously, the more people there are sharing a home, the more potential there is for stress, but also, the stage is set for sharing, and for a wider exchange of knowledge and love. Whatever style of family you live in, you will have to deal with some or all of the following problems.

Conflict

Let's look at some case studies involving conflicts between parents and their teenage children, reflecting the things that cause your teenagers, and consequently you, the most stress. *Problem: Disobedience and 'cheek'.* A mother has to deal with her thirteen-year-old son suddenly giving her 'cheek', answering back, defying her, being disobedient. This has not been part of his previous behaviour pattern. She feels at a loss to deal with it. Should she come down hard and tell him in no uncertain terms that she isn't going to put up with it, or should she give him a bit of rope and let things find their own level? *Solution:* I'd be inclined to try the latter for a short time. The boy needs to know his boundaries, the line over which he must not cross. But some leeway needs to be allowed, at least until the highly volatile situation settles down. The boundary has to be communicated to him very clearly, by saying, for example: 'The next time you swear at me, you'll be punished.' These conditions must then be applied, without exception. If

2 Your Home

Many of you will have picked up this book in a desperate attempt to reach a better understanding of your teenage boy or girl. You've probably heard and learnt enough over the years to write a book yourself, but when it got to your turn, when your beloved children became that dreaded thing, teenagers!, you found that all the lessons and advice prepared you not a jot. Does this describe it pretty well? If it does, you may feel better when I tell you that you are by no means alone. I surveyed all my friends who are parents of teenagers and, without exception, the main reaction was a mixture of conflict and confusion.

Many conflicting emotions come into play, including nostalgia for the past, for the simple, sweet children you once had; feelings of loss as your teenagers back away from you more and more, starting with 'Don't kiss me in front of my friends, Mum' to not telling you their secrets any more and then excluding you from their lives, making you feel archaic, ignorant, boring; and frustration, as you no longer know how to communicate with them — whatever you say seems to be the wrong thing, and you feel the chasm between yourself and your teenager grow wider and wider each day. Sorry to make it sound so grim. Some of you will have it far worse than this and others slightly better.

In many Australian homes there is Mum, Dad and the kids,

11

10 ■ TEENAGE STRESS

- Handling authority and what is seen as the 'system'
- Biological changes and pressures
- Juggling school, home, sometimes, work and personal pressures
- All the usual things that plague their adult counterparts as well, such as deadlines, noise, traffic, money problems, work demands
- Emergence of sexual feelings, dealing with the opposite sex, dating

Having looked at the issues of stress in a general way, let's move now to the stress management procedures for teenagers and coping techniques for their parents, which I have covered in this book, chapter by chapter.

THE NATURE OF STRESS ■ 9

accepted passively, when passions run hot and fear is unknown. Perhaps I need to clarify a point here: on the one hand, teenagers are fearless, on the other, they're petrified. This dilemma sums up a basic challenge for teenagers: their lives are full of contradictions.

When we see a teenager giving cheek to a teacher, all we see is a young person 'being rude'. While the rudeness can never be justified, it often represents a cry for help. Let's face it, teachers are not perfect beings. Some abuse their power, use 'dark sarcasm in the classroom', as the song says, humiliate and belittle their students and are more concerned with their own egos than with teaching. What comeback does a student have after prolonged unfair treatment? Sometimes, young people will explode as stress upon stress piles up; even the most patient and tolerant teenager can 'freak out'. As with adult stress, it doesn't always manifest in the appropriate manner and setting. If teenagers could be rational and mature in dealing with their conflicts, they wouldn't be teenagers. So, frustrations and built-up anger in the classroom may show up days later in the home. I was never rude to the nuns who taught me, despite the various injustices of a typical Catholic convent education, but I was certainly unreasonable and difficult at home at times.

I remember one particular incident when I was about fifteen. A girlfriend and I were not participating in a sports day one Sunday and so arrived in our 'civvies'. Nothing happened until the next morning when we were called out of class to explain our 'bold behaviour'. I was accused of wearing a 'low-cut evening gown', which was in fact a high-necked summer dress! It's funny to look back on now, but when you have to stand at attention and get dressed-down for something you feel you haven't done, it's very humiliating at any age but excruciating for a teenager who has a heightened sense of outrage, especially as it applies to personal pride.

To sum up, teenage stress is caused mainly by:
■ The very nature of teenage
■ Coping with normal home and family issues

8 ■ TEENAGE STRESS

Teenagers encourage each other to smoke, experiment with drugs, drink too much alcohol, give cheek to teachers and thumb their noses at the so-called system. Most go along, and pay the high price for the most desirable commodity in any teenager's life: acceptance. Those on the fringe, for whatever reasons, eventually give up and live the lonely life of not belonging. Young people can be rejected for their looks, their clothes, for being too studious, too quiet, too respectful, and sometimes for no apparent reason at all. Many teenagers who contemplate or commit suicide cite rejection and loneliness as their reason. It's a time when defects stand out, self-esteem is at its lowest ebb and popularity most prized. The stress traps in this arena are numerous and will be looked at in detail in chapter 3.

Problems with learning are a rich source of stressful feelings and pressures. The naturally bright and beautiful have both ends working for them, but most teenagers will either be popular and less academic or studious loners. I don't know of any studies in Australia that have looked at this area of research, perhaps because abstract concepts such as popularity are hard to pin down, but it certainly would unearth some interesting statistics, I'm sure. It's a question of time and energy, and focus — most teenagers have to juggle so many balls in the air that they end up deciding what they're best at and sticking to it. For some, their talent might be simply being the class clown, for others, being good at sport wins acclaim, yet others excel at academic pursuits, and the majority worship at the altar of being one of the gang, of not standing out. Yet, somehow, exams have to be taken, assignments tackled, grades faced up to. There's only so much bluffing and avoiding and getting by that can be done. So schoolwork is a major stress area for teenagers.

And, finally, there are potential problems with teachers, principals and rules. The very nature of a teenager causes him/her to rebel, question, defy. While it's infuriating for adults, it's absolutely essential for young people to go through this stage. In some cases, it's the only time when life is not simply

THE NATURE OF STRESS ■ 7

violence — the possibilities, and combinations, are endless. There's no point in expecting a teenager to make concessions to whatever else is going on in the family, because at this point in life, he/she is liable to be totally egocentric and self-absorbed. One of the chief causes of conflict in homes with a teenager is the insistence on the part of a parent that the young person act responsibly and rationally. A reasonable analogy would be someone asking a lion to sit down quietly and eat dinner; that person shouldn't complain if he ends up *being* dinner. It's the nature of the beast.

Boundaries on behaviour can of course be set, but there should be a wide margin given for rebellion and defiance. Being a teenager is hard enough and being the parent of a teenager is hard enough without overly-prescriptive attitudes being brought into play. It's a case of 'less is more'.

So, at home, parental attitudes are crucial when it comes to the amount of stress being generated. Matters such as whether or not the teenager is praised for work well done, loved unconditionally, given the precious gift of time and being listened to, encouraged to learn and take risks in life, given a reasonable amount of responsibility in the home together with large doses of flexibility are vital. Their absence will create tremendous emotional stress which then rebounds on the family as a whole.

Of course, the teenager's own attitude is pivotal to this issue as well. All teenagers have much in common, but some will be more amenable, pleasant, emotional, hardworking, et cetera. than others. While the more placid and the more positive ones might agonise over the same key problems, they may not be as vulnerable to stress simply because of their personalities. But whatever the personality traits, there are many areas of a person's life that can be adapted and improved. That's why stress management techniques are so important.

School

At school, most teenage stress generates from three areas: peer pressure, problems with study, and conflict with authority figures.

6 ■ TEENAGE STRESS

to endure another unendurable day. If it feels as if you've lost your child, it's because, to a large extent, you have. They are out of your reach for a time. What I aim to do in this book is help you to gain a little more understanding of the teenage psyche, which is, essentially, in constant stress. I can suggest the whys and the hows, why we suffer stress and how to make it better, but unfortunately, I have no magic formula to make all the pain go away. Anyway, who says that would necessarily be a desirable thing? Pain is what keeps us alive and on our toes.

The key is management, making sure the scales tip in our favour so that there's more good stuff than bad stuff in our lives. During the course of this book, I will cheer you with reminders of all the wonderful things that teenagers are: as well as infuriating, maddening, frustrating, impossible, they are also refreshing, honest, straightforward, fascinating and a never-ending source of surprises.

Causes of teenage stress

What causes teenagers to be under too much stress? In brief, the main causes are: the very nature of the teenage years; coping with normal home and family issues; handling authority and what is seen as 'the system'; biological changes and pressures; juggling school, home, sometimes work, and personal pressures; emergence of sexual feelings, dealing with the opposite sex, dating; uncertainty about the future. Plus, all the everyday problems that plague adults as well, such as deadlines, noise, traffic, money problems, work demands.

Home

A difficult family life (and by difficult, I mean unhappy) can have a variety of causes. Even the most tranquil home can be devastated by Typhoon Teenager, so imagine one in which Dad might just have been retrenched, Mum is menopausal, there are financial problems, a bunch of younger children in a too-small house, perhaps problems connected with alcohol or

THE NATURE OF STRESS ■ 5

Teenage should really be called 'tweenage' because it's like being on a bridge, crossing from one existence to another, yet being forever in limbo, not belonging in either world. If this seems a very dramatic description, it seems so only in recollection, not in the experience, which is more wonderful and more terrifying than words could ever say. Nothing can ever really diminish these extremes, and perhaps that is as it should be. We each have to cross that bridge and, ultimately, we are alone, but there is one vital weapon that we can take with us: knowledge. With knowledge and awareness, we can feel comforted and brave in the face of adversity — and that's where a book like this one comes in.

Stress and teenagers

With teenagers, it's not a case of identifying stress symptoms, it's more a matter of deciding which ones are the most pronounced. It might even be accurate to say that 'stress' and 'teenage' are synonomous.

What we can judge, however, is the level at which an individual teenager is under stress. This is a very subtle exercise and requires a good deal of practice. Of course, the long-suffering parent is the one who has to decide when the bout of sulking has gone on too long or what the warning signs are when a teenager's depression has become too severe; when to nag, cajole or enquire, and when to say nothing. But history tells us that many, many times, parents misjudge these signs and are faced with the lifelong guilt of a depressed child who commits suicide without, seemingly, any warning; the son or daughter who is discovered to have been taking drugs for years or to be an alcoholic; the pregnant daughter, the violent son. No wonder so many parents despair of the task when their beloved children grow into 'monsters' during that long night between twelve and thirteen.

Parents, when you are about ready to give up, remember that bridge and your child alone upon it — it may help you

Physical

Physical symptoms include chronic headache, insomnia, tightness in the chest and other parts of the body, chronic fatigue. Tension can be stored in the body and manifest itself as unexplained aches and pains.

Emotional

Emotional reactions to stress can result in relationship breakdown, chronic depression, irritability, mood swings, loss of interest in sex and closeness of all kinds, arguing and quarrelling.

Mental

Stress can cause mental problems such as loss of concentration, poor work performance, loss of memory, difficulty in making decisions, confusion, over-sensitivity.

For teenagers, the same symptoms apply but are usually more extreme. The hormonal changes and developments that rage in the teenage body cause almost constant sensations of stress. Restlessness, grouchiness, erratic moods, crying, depression — these are all everyday companions for the teenager, and must be endured along with the other, already considerable, burdens of growing up.

There is nothing I can say that will minimise the complexity of this time in a person's life. For some teenagers, it's not all bad; for others, every day is a sojourn to the mouth of the volcano. It's no wonder so many want to jump in. There are challenges at every stage of every human life, but I think it's the concentration of problems during teenage which makes it a time most of us shudder to remember. In most cases, the memory is bitter-sweet. We remember acne but also the wonder of our first kiss; feeling ugly and alone but also wonderfully free; the thousand conflicting emotions, the heartbreak of first love, the anger and the ecstasy of being so close to adulthood yet as lost and scared as a child.

working plates as much as possible. Then, they're surprised when they become too stressed to work or worse still, suffer a severe stress attack.

No, you do not have to be unduly stressed in order to do good work. You need enough stress to get you motivated, but to work continually under pressure is very wearing on the human body. It breaks down the immune system and makes us more prone to disease. That's why, when people get sick, they'll often say they've been feeling 'run down'.

If you're by nature a stressful person, you can learn to manage your habit

If you are by nature a stressful person, it simply means that you have a particular personality type which is characterised by being an over-achiever, compulsive, a perfectionist, over-anxious, hardworking. This type of personality will almost always be prone to over-do in most areas of life, with habits that attract stress — for instance, taking work home too often, or having a messy desk so that finding every little item is a stress event. I am a recovered stressaholic and can testify to the addictive nature of stress. It's a complex issue that will be explained during the course of this book. The best expert is one who has been through it. Everything I tell you about is based on personal experience. You can change!

Remember, stress is a cause *and* a consequence. It has a circular effect and is very insidious. Its harmful effects accumulate unseen, and that's why prevention is your best weapon against it.

The symptoms of stress

How do you know when you're living with too much stress in your life? I'll discuss the most common symptoms and then relate them specifically to teenagers.

2 ■ TEENAGE STRESS

playing sport, taking a driving test, and undertaking similar tasks. Without stress, we would never get up in the mornings. So there *is* such a thing as too little stress! In this book, you will see that if it is harnessed properly, stress can actually be a friend and an ally.

Stress is a modern phenomenon

Stress has been part of human life ever since people first walked the planet. If it appears to be a modern disease, it's only because we talk about it so much more now. Humans have exposed much more of their vulnerability to each other in recent decades, in a whole range of areas. Previously unheard-of topics are now freely aired. Who would have believed, a few years ago, that we would see ads on television selling condoms and tampons, that there would be entire television shows devoted to people airing their dirty linen in public, that stories of incest and rape could be considered prime-time entertainment? Society seems to have a hunger for the more sordid aspects of life, fed by the media, and 'stress' is just an umbrella term for all the harshness, pain and suffering that are part of human existence.

People now exchange stress stories the way they once told each other about their operations. Some actually boast of breakdowns and 'burnout'. One of the things I will be explaining in this book is that it's possible to become a stress junkie, so take all the hype with a grain of salt. It's not clever to go into stress overload, and it *is* avoidable. It's all a matter of balance.

Stress is necessary to 'get the job done'

There is a belief held by a lot of people, especially those who do creative work, that they cannot work except under pressure, so they drive themselves for long hours at a stretch, eat erratically and poorly, hardly sleep and try to overfill their

1 The Nature of Stress

Before anything else, we need to look at the nature of stress itself and how it relates to teenagers in particular. 'Stress' is a word we hear often these days but misconceptions abound as to what it really is. Stress is the external force of pressure that we feel when we're busy, tired or rushed. Sometimes we can cause internal stress in ourselves, but I prefer to make a distinction and call this internal stress 'tension'. So, throughout this book, the terms used are stress for external pressure and tension for internal pressure.

Myths

Many myths surround ideas about stress. Let's take these each in turn, and examine them.

Stress is always a bad or negative thing

Stress is by no means always a negative thing. Athletes and performers of many kinds could not reach the heights of success and glory if they were totally unstressed. We all need an adrenalin rush to give us the impetus to get on with our daily lives, especially when taking exams, going for a job interview,

Beautiful unlined faces,
like blank pages
waiting to be written upon,
eager young minds
thirsting for knowledge and truth,
healthy bodies
crying out for love.
They call it youth.
I remember it
as the confusion
of living somewhere
between heaven and hell . . .

NANUSHKA

This book is dedicated to all my students, past and present. Thank you for the joy you brought to my life, the love you left in my heart, and for teaching me much more than I ever taught you.

one, have a deep and genuine love and respect for teenagers, as will be evident through the pages of this book. In many ways, writing this book was a sentimental journey for me as I remembered my own childhood years and all the wonderful classrooms of girls that I knew during my years as a secondary school teacher.

Let us now embark on this journey together, a journey of sharing, discovery and hope. I received some very lovely letters from readers of *Women and Stress*, some from as far away as England. In the hope that the same thing will happen with this book, I include here my postal address for your comments, ideas, questions. I promise to write back to you and help in whatever way I can.

Box 637
Subiaco WA 6008

Foreword

One of the main questions I was asked about my last book, *Women and Stress*, was — why is it necessary to write about the stress of only one section of society? Is female stress really different? No doubt the same issue will be raised about *Teenage Stress*. My answer will be the same: the stress itself is essentially the same, but how it manifests and how it is experienced varies according to gender, age, background, personality.

Having worked with teenagers off and on for over twenty years, I have many wonderful memories, stories and insights, some of which I plan to share with you in this book. My main aim is to offer a comprehensive study of teenage stress for the use of young men and women and their parents. The story will unfold via description, anecdotes, case studies and, most importantly, a positive and practical approach to the special challenges of growing up in the 'between' years.

I cannot hope to discuss every teenage issue in detail, and, in order to say anything at all, I have to take the middle road and leave out mention of Aboriginal or migrant teenagers, the handicapped or the brilliant, those with very unusual and specific problems. My premise is that all teenagers share the same feelings, frustrations and fears to some extent, and these cross all boundaries of culture, race, language, intellect and other differences. I hope, therefore, that this book will have something to say to all young people and their families. I, for

Contents

The Nature of Stress 1

Your Home 11

School 23

Sexuality 30

Emotions 38

Health 48

Work and Employment 54

Personal Growth 60

Agencies teenagers can call on 71

Books for parents and teenagers 72

Acknowledgments

I would firstly like to thank Sally Milner, my publisher, without whose support this book may not have been written.

Also, my cat, Max, who kept me company during the many lonely hours in front of the computer.

Fran Head of the Down to Earth bookshop in Perth, who supplied the reading list, and organised a WA launch for the book.

The Citizens' Advice Bureau in Bunbury, WA, who helped me with information about agencies that help adolescents.

Ann Poublon of Dymock's bookshops, WA, who has given me support and encouragement with the marketing of all my books, and who has generously arranged a seminar around this current publication.

No book is a solo effort. I take this opportunity to thank all my colleagues, friends and supporters who have contributed directly and indirectly to the writing of this book and the information contained herein.

About the Author

Charmaine Saunders has been working in the personal development field since 1983. As a counsellor, author, teacher and columnist, she has gained a wide following because of her practical, down-to-earth advice and outgoing personality.

She has written two previous books about stress and writes a weekly advice column for a West Australian newspaper, as well as regular articles for magazines and other publications. Her popular 'Ask Charmaine' segments on ABC Radio and commercial stations are entertaining as well as informative. Her busy schedule includes marketing a series of personal development tapes, operating a mail friendship club and running a counselling practice. She has brought her warmth and humour as well as her vast experience and knowledge to the writing of *Teenage Stress.*

Teenage Stress

Teenagers live in a world of change and confusion. There are stress traps in family life, school, work, relationships, just growing up. More than every today, young people need help and guidance to get them through the years between childhood and adulthood. Teenage suicide is on the increase, youth unemployment is at an all-time high, family life is breaking down. How do we teach teenagers to stay positive through all these challenges?

Dr Charmaine Saunders is a columnist, teacher and counsellor who has worked with young people for over twenty years. In this, her third stress book, she offers practical strategies, positive advice and down-to-earth ideas about teenage life, both for parents and teenagers themselves. Through case studies, anecdotes, examples and exercises, she leads the reader with humour, warmth and, most importantly, hope.

This book is a must for all teenagers, their parents and anyone who has a professional and personal interest in the welfare of young people and their future role in society.

First published in 1992 by
Sally Milner Publishing Pty Ltd
558 Darling Street
Rozelle NSW 2039 Australia

© Charmaine Saunders 1992

Production by Sylvana Scannapiego,
Island Graphics
Typeset in Australia by Asset Typesetting Pty Ltd
Printed in Australia by Australian Print Group

National Library of Australia
Cataloguing-in-Publication data:

Saunders, Charmaine.
    Teenage stress.

    ISBN 1 86351 088 5.

    1. Stress in adolescence. 2. Stress (Psychology).
    3. Teenagers — Health and hygiene. I. Title.
    (Series: Milner healthy living guide).

155.90420835

All rights reserved. No part of this publication may be
reproduced, stored in a retrieval system or transmitted in
any form or by any means, electronic, mechanical,
photocopying, recording or otherwise, without prior
written permission of the copyright owners and publishers.

teenage STRESS

A Guide for Parents

Dr Charmaine Saunders

SALLY MILNER PUBLISHING

teenage
STRESS
A Guide for Parents